Resurgence

Navigating the Changing Ministry Landscape

Candace M. Lewis

Rodney Thomas Smothers

Drs. Candace Lewis and Rodney Smothers make a splendidly unique offering in "Resurgence." With honor for the past, and even reverence, the analysis and prescriptive principles and tools they present in this text promise fresh creativity and renewed ministry for the future. Try this book's ideas and strategies to find vital possibilities emerging in your congregation.

Vance P. Ross, Senior Pastor
Central United Methodist Church, Atlanta, GA

Many resources have been written, however this book/workbook provides the kind of probing questions, examples and life experiences if resurgence is to happen. If the church is to be revitalized, restored, renewed, regenerated, this resource will guide leaders to ask the hard question as to whether we live or die.

Rev. Geraldine W. McClellan
Retired United Methodist Church Elder, Gainesville, Florida

Resurgence will transform the way African American congregations see themselves. Candace and Rodney use their rich experiences to challenge, guide, encourage and implore congregations to a new understanding of what it means to be a leader. Readers will learn how to build bridges between generations while moving a congregation toward new vitality.

F. Douglas Powe, Jr., Ph.D.
Director of Lewis Center for Church Leadership
Wesley Theological Seminary

Dr. Lewis and Smothers are certainly on to something with this book as they courageously challenge church leaders to engage rather than avoid the societal changes impacting the local church. Their positive attitude towards the potential for significant transformation in the life of congregations willing to risk traveling on new pathways is needed and refreshing. As a local pastor and a denominational leader, this book will provide practical solutions through the discovery of best practices from churches who have themselves experienced a fresh wind of resurgence. Dr. Lewis and Smothers book will certainly have an impact on the Kingdom.

Rev. Dr. Wayne D. Faison
Senior Pastor, East End Baptist Church – Suffolk, VA

RESURGENCE

Navigating the Changing
Ministry Landscape

Candace M. Lewis
Rodney Thomas Smothers

CONTENTS

Acknowledgments

All things are possible to she who believes! I am thankful to my mom, Mrs. Cora Lewis, for her prayers and encouragement throughout this book project. I'm grateful to my siblings, girl-friends, friends, and colleagues for your ongoing support. We did it! Thank you, Johnny Stephens and Grassroots Publishing, for your partnership. Special thanks to Beverly Sonnier for your invest-ment of time and energy in editing this project. Thanks, Cedric Lewis, for your writing contributions, and L.K. Rich, for cover design and writing contributions. Thank you to my New Life family for enabling me to live out my call as a pastor and a church planter. I'm grateful to Bishop Vaughn McLaughlin and the Potter's House Pastors Class for offering me space to ask questions and learn that pastors can improve in authentic, accountable community. Thank you to the Path1 Church Planting staff, team, and movement for giving me an opportunity to become a national coach, consul-tant, and resource person. Thank you, Bishop Ken Carter and the Florida Cabinet and Conference, for inviting me to serve and share my ministry gifts as a missional strategist.

— Candace Lewis

To God be the glory! I am thankful for all of the congregations that I have served as pastor and the pastors and laity who have allowed me to come alongside them and serve as their coach. My fellow congregational developers and the community of authors, bloggers, podcasters, and workshop leaders have fed my spirit and challenged my thinking. Colleagues in the North Georgia and Baltimore-Washington conferences of The United Methodist Church have provided me the laboratory to implement the ideas contained in this book. This journey would not have been possible without the reflections of my children, Jasmine, Jason, and Laken, who have also served as travelers on this journey. Dr. Lynn Thomas Smothers, my wife, has been a blessing as an encourager, reviewer, and prayer partner in seeing this book to publication.

— Rodney Thomas Smothers

Foreword

I have learned over time that when I am in the presence of gifted and creative leaders who have a demonstrated history of transformation on several levels, I want to listen closely. I want to lean in.

Candace Lewis and Rodney Smothers are two of our movement's most compelling advocates for the renewal of the church. They reflect in these pages on the black church, but I would urge the reader not to place them and what they are offering us in a box. This is a rich offering, the fruit of a long and faithful labor, a sacrifice acceptable and pleasing to God. It arises from the experience of planting new churches, serving cross cultural congregations, and designing systems of leadership at every level of the church.

The resurgence they imagine for the church is about renewal, revival and recovery of relevancy among leaders and the people among whom they serve. They know our past, they see the present with clarity, but they have also peered into the future that is already breaking out among us. They are clear about the shifts we will need to consider if we are to experience resurgence.

Among these are:
- general changes affecting the black church and its place in society
- the pervasiveness of the digital culture
- the political transition from the Civil Rights Movement to Black Lives Matter
- the priority of catalytic leadership over caretaking
- the essential shift from heroic solo leadership to team ministry
- the power of asking questions in coaching relationships

- a real conversation about funding, generosity, and resources
- why membership is less important than discipleship systems

Lewis and Smothers weave together their own stories, the theory underneath these dynamic changes in the landscape, and questions and tools that will help individuals and teams or leaders to process this in their own settings.

Someone once told me that a mediocre coach tells a team to win. An extraordinary coach helps the players to engage in the habits, behaviors, mindsets, and practices that will actually help them to win. The church is in a fragile state, and the black church is an essential part of this ecosystem. We cannot continue to use the same playbook. We cannot remain committed to the same assumptions about effectiveness and success. We cannot look to models that worked 20 to 50 years ago as the path to resurgence.

Nostalgia will not be of great help to us. What is most helpful is seeing the reality of where we are; drawing upon the rich and deep faith of the black church; and with appreciation for all that has been, having the courage and creativity to step into God's future. Candace Lewis and Rodney Smothers are leaders with a deep faith in Jesus Christ and love for his church. They love the church—and the appropriate focus here is the black church, which called them and which they have blessed—but one must quickly say that they love the church enough to speak truth in love about the present reality and our resistance to change. This book is about how to overcome the status quo through new habits, behaviors, mindsets, and practices.

God wants to give us a gift, and that is resurgence: revival, renewal, relevance.

I have listened closely to what Dr. Lewis and Pastor Smothers are teaching me. I invite you into this conversation. It is needed. I hope leaders in many of our churches will walk alongside their pastors in learning from the wisdom of this book.

Ken Carter
President, Council of Bishops, The United Methodist Church
Resident Bishop, Florida Conference

What Is Resurgence?

Is your church making a significant difference in relevant mission or ministry? As a leader, are you seeking to know how to lead into the future? What would a fresh wind that rejuvenates a declining congregation, navigating societal shifts, look and feel like?

One word: Resurgence.

Resurgence is the next season of transformation the church can experience. It is the identification of a new skill set called "navigating" that will help you discover best practices and new pathways that create new life in once vital congregations. by helping you interrupt the congregational decline, and understand the societal shifts that are requiring pastors and leaders to lead differently.

Through this resource, we will act as that fresh wind of rejuvenation blowing through your church. We will resource you to lead renewal, assist you in "navigating" the current ministry landscape and lead transformational change that can bring new life and vitality to churches and communities.What is *resurgence?* It is a term that we have chosen to describe the next season of transformation the church can experience. Resurgence *strategies* assist you in navigating the current ministry landscape, and resurgence *principles* assist you in leading transformational change that can bring new life and vitality to churches and communities.

What is *resurgence?* It is the identification of a new skill set called "navigating" that will help you discover best practices and new pathways that create new life in once vital congregations. Resurgence is a fresh wind that rejuvenates declining congregations by creating new strategies for reversing congregational decline and providing strategies for renewal and new life.

This resource has developed out of our labor of love for the local church. Collectively, we now have over 50 years of experience as pastors, denominational leaders, strategists, consultants, and coaches. The one thing that arises from all of those vantage points is that the ministry of the local church continues to evolve and the pace of evolution and change is occurring much faster than most of us as adults have experienced. Yet, when we attend worship service on Sunday mornings, although comfortable and familiar, it may seem as if we've entered a time warp of sorts.

Many of our churches are slow to adapt and make changes to engage the times in which we are living—today. We celebrate these churches as they offer an experience that is enjoyable to the people that currently attend. We are asking these churches to examine their current ministry setting and effectiveness in strengthening existing disciples and reaching new people.

This resource addresses significant landmarks and suggests future benchmarks for continuing vital and trans-formational local church ministries. We have identified a current starting point and seek to assist churches in navigat-ing to a next and new place in their church's journey. We believe that churches can experience a new season of resur-gence. By definition, it begins with a defined starting point and evolves through an ongoing journey. The outcome of resurgence is a new season of life, vitality, and kingdom impact within the congregation that overflows into the community.

Let the journey begin!

Navigating the Changing Ministry Landscape

"There's a season for everything and a time for every matter under the heavens." – Ecclesiastes 3:1 (CEB)

"Change is the law of life and those who look only to the past or present are certain to miss the future." – John F. Kennedy

A re We There Yet? is a movie about the adventures that occur on a family vacation. "Are we there yet?" is also a question that many children and non-drivers ask on a trip. They are glad about the travel progress while anxiously anticipating arriving at the destination. As the trip unfolds, the passengers glance out the window with excitement about where they are and how soon they'll get there. They ask, *"Are we there yet?"* It doesn't matter that it's only been ten minutes since the last time they asked, the question is asked over and over again until they can see the journey is over and they have reached their destination.

Have you ever been on vacation with family, friends, children, or grandchildren and been asked, "Are we there yet?"

Airlines recognize how important it is for people to gauge the progress of the trip and project the amount of time remaining. Whenever travelers wonder, *Are we there yet?*

on a newer aircraft or on most international flights, passengers can check the moving map that tells them the distance traveled and the distance remaining before they arrive.

I (Candace) recently flew from Seattle to South Carolina. The next day, I traveled to Detroit to lead a training event. On both flights, I found myself frequently checking the moving map because I simply wanted to know "Are we there yet?"

Travelers and passengers ask this question because they are aware that they are on a journey. They may have an estimated time of arrival, but they do not have an exact arrival time. Navigational tools continue to help travelers in arriving successfully to their desired destinations. Whether you are using a compass, a paper map or an electronic map, or a satellite-based GPS system, navigational tools can be helpful.

Through this resource, we seek to help you discover valuable navigational tools as you lead, serve, and seek to understand the new ministry terrain of the church in general and the black church in particular.

Understanding Ministry Landmarks and Landscapes

While riding in a car, today's passengers often occupy themselves with phones and other electronic devices equipped with games, movies, and music. Conversation and periodic daydreaming while looking out the window also occupy their time. On a long, picturesque trip, they have the opportunity to take in historic landmarks and appreciate emerging landscapes, often seeing both at the same time.

Landmarks can be defined as historic or geographically significant places in past history and present experiences. *Landscapes* may be described as emerging places and spaces filled with potential, just awaiting discovery and development.

As church leaders, we too are able to see landmarks and landscapes along our leadership journey. We often have to choose whether we will focus our leadership time, effort, and energy on maintaining the landmarks or engaging the emerging ministry landscape opportunities.

What Do You See?

Landmarks and landscapes may await development in and outside of the church relevant to your ministry context. Many leaders have a strong sense of call and a desire to engage their current and emerging ministry landscape. It's also important for church leaders to recognize and name current ministry landscape opportunities.

Resurgent leaders learn the importance of assessing and naming the current realities of their ministry context. Using the Asset-Mapping tool will help leaders see the assets and liabilities of their respective ministry context along with the landscape and landmarks within the community.

When leaders see primarily with a landmark view of ministry, the focus is frequently only on maintenance of existing buildings, programs, policies, and problems the church continues to experience. The landmarks have to be acknowledged and addressed to clear the way to see the landscape surrounding and ahead.

A landscape view helps leaders not only see the needs of current and existing members but also the people not connected to Christ or the church. Your desire and passion to engage them also begins to grow.

Get Ready to Lead a Resurgence: Navigating the Ministry Landscape

If someone told you 25 years ago that you would carry around at all times a phone in your pocket or purse and that you would be able to use it to access information almost instantly, would you have believed them? Most of us did not envision this type of rapid change in technology and probably did not see ourselves adapting as often as we have to it. But just think about how many times you've upgraded your phone in the last five years.

Our phones are a good example of how things evolve and change and how we can adapt to these changes. From its beginning as a device through which to play music to its seemingly unlimited capabilities today, the smartphone has become an indispensable tool for many things in our lives.

Similar to how our phones have evolved fundamentally as a communication device, a church that's ready to create and experience resurgence understands the church exists for the maintenance of worship, the edification of believers, and the redemption of the world.[1] This foundational purpose of the church does not change, but the way in which the church engages its current ministry context can evolve with the times.

A resurgent church understands its purpose and builds on something that has worked well while applying innovation in ways that significantly make a difference. Resurgence in the church begins and ends with taking the tried and true and improving it for the current and emerging ministry settings where we serve.

What Is Resurgence?

For the purposes of this resource, we define resurgence as a movement toward renewal, revival, and recovery of relevancy in ministry today among leaders and churches. When we engage in resurgence we:

- reclaim relevancy in our congregations and communities.
- re-vision ministries to engage current and future people needs.
- realign and add value to assets by creatively repurposing church space.
- redefine current leadership and church assumptions, models, and approaches by asking and answering more relevant questions.

---

1 *The Book of Discipline of The United Methodist Church,* 2016; page 147.

- reconnect with our call and commitment to Christ and Christ's church in a post-Christian and pluralistic society.

Through resurgence, leaders and churches are invited to discover again the "why" of ministry and to reconnect with passion and purpose in our current ministry context. Resurgence is the opportunity to "re" (meaning back or again) in the midst of our current ministry and to imagine our future destination as a church.

Why Is Resurgence Needed Now?

Many of life's critical systems are undergoing close scrutiny and examination to determine if they have outlived their usefulness in their current state. These systems include economics, education, politics, transportation, technology, employment, and religion. When viewed as a system, the black church is not exempt from such scrutiny. It, too, should be examined for opportunities to be retooled for increased relevance or risk being sidelined and labeled irrelevant and obsolete.

For some, seeing and experiencing these systems change and shift in our lifetime can be scary. Much of the change feels imposed upon us, and our natural human tendency in the face of imposed change is to fight or flee. The fight response is seen in churches that become embroiled in conflicts and infighting over insignificant issues, which often is easier than wrestling with the honest challenges of an uncertain future. We are writing this book to reassure church leaders that the future can be faced unafraid. For over 2,000 years, the church has adapted and changed.

In her book *The Great Emergence*, Phyllis Tickle says, "Like every 'new season,' this one we recognize as the Great Emergence affects every part of our lives. In its totality, it interfaces with, and is the context for, everything we do socially, culturally, intellectually, politically, economically."[2]

---

2 *The Great Emergence*, by Phyllis Tickle (Baker Books, 2012); page 2.

This resource acknowledges change at our doorstep. We can no longer ignore the knocking and continue to do business as usual. It's time to open the door of our minds, hearts, and the church to the opportunity to experience resurgence. If we choose to remain closed to this new reality, it will be difficult, if not impossible, for the church as we know it to have a future.

Noted author and motivational speaker Simon Sinek explores how leaders can inspire cooperation, trust, and change. His classic book *Start With Why* begins with a series of fundamental questions[3]:

- Why are some people and organizations more innovative, more influential, and more profitable than others?
- Why do some command greater loyalty from customers and employees alike?
- Even among the successful, why are so few able to repeat their success over and over?

People like Martin Luther King Jr., Steve Jobs, and the Wright Brothers had little in common, but they all started with a "why." They realized that people would not buy into a product, service, movement, or idea until they understood the "why" behind it. So before you decide whether or not to take action, consider why and how using these resources and simple strategies can engage and stimulate your current and future ministries.

Understanding Societal Shifts

This book acknowledges that the pace of change in the church is happening so quickly that a resource in navigating these changes is needed. Using a navigation metaphor, this resource will assist pastors and leaders in understanding the concept that current and future ministry context

---

3 *Start With Why*, by Simon Sinek (Portfolio Penquin Publishing Group, 1976).

acknowledges: A good navigation system is connected to a satellite that gives you real-time information.

Most of us use GPS systems., but many of us might not know exactly what it is. The global positioning system (GPS) is a 24-satellite navigation system that uses multiple satellite signals to find a receiver's position on earth. Once you enter in your destination on a GPS device or app, it will give your starting point and provide directions for you to reach your destination.

We might not fully understand how these devices work, but we trust our lives and livelihood to them every day. Why? Because they provide context and convenience to our coming and going. These devices enhance our ability to think and to make decisions.

This resource is not about "experts" offering a single methodology to renewal. Instead, through this resource, we are:

- providing tools that assist pastors and leaders in discovering forward-thinking strategies that uniquely fit their individual church and ministry contexts.
- assisting pastors and leaders in navigating the uncertain terrain toward a relevant and vital future.
- understanding that the gift of navigating the terrain comes with clear options.
- challenging pastors and leaders to make critical decisions. (Will you continue to trust only your instincts about the best future direction of the church? Or will you become open to considering current changes, available information, and insights from other sources?)
- challenging pastors and leaders to consider new paths and options instead of staying on one path simply because "that's the way we've always done it." This resource is about suspending judgment momentarily to see how you and your

ministry can benefit from this resource.

- inviting pastors and leaders to learn more about evolving landscapes and to consider more than one path leading to their desired destination.

The Authors' Stories

Candace

When I was a child, my parents did not attend church, so my grandmother was actively involved in my early faith formation. I remember when Mama (as we affectionately called my grandmother) came to the house and said to my mother, "These kids need to go to church." She said that she would pick us up Saturday and take us shopping to buy church clothes. I still remember putting on the beautiful black patent-leather shoes she bought me and getting my hair pressed the night before, all because I was going to church with Mama Sunday morning.

Wearing a pretty new dress and new shoes, and with my hair freshly pressed, I was on my way to church along with my siblings. At six years old, I had no idea what church was, but I knew it must be an important place because only special people and a special occasion merited getting new clothes and shoes. Although I did not understand all that occurred during worship, I was aware that it was a place of hope and possibilities. People laughed, cried, sang, served, and had great dinners after church in the annex or outside on the grass.

After two years at Mount Calvary, my aunt invited us to attend the new St. John Missionary Baptist Church. They had church every Sunday. She believed it was important for me and my siblings to be in Sunday school each week in order for us to grow as Christians.

When I was 12, my father had a conversion experience and decided that the entire family would attend church together. We joined Zion United Methodist Church, the only black United Methodist church in our community. I served in various leadership capacities while a member of Zion and was nurtured by faithful women and men who encouraged me to love and serve the Lord.

Throughout my life, I've responded to the call to lead. I consider leadership to be an honor and a responsibility. I received an undergraduate degree from the University of Florida, majoring in speech communications. Upon graduation, I was awarded the Distinguished Outstanding Female Student Leader award for excellent service in leadership.

I answered my call to ministry; and at the age of 22, I obediently followed God and enrolled in Gammon Theological Seminary in Atlanta, Georgia. Four years later, I received the master of divinity degree with a concentration in pastoral care and counseling.

That same year, I traveled to South Africa and Zimbabwe to participate in a biblical studies program. Three years later, I participated in the John Wesley study program in London, England, followed by participation in the Harvard Divinity School's summer leadership institute on faith-based community economic development. I traveled to Hong Kong, China, and Accra, Ghana, in West Africa as a mission ministry team member. Later, I was elected by my peers to serve as a delegate to General Conference and the Southeastern Jurisdictional Conference of The United Methodist Church.

My experiences in and passion for effective leadership did not end there. I am an ordained elder in the Florida Annual Conference of The United Methodist Church and founding pastor of New Life Community United Methodist Church in Jacksonville, Florida, where I served for 13 years. The church started in June 1997 with seven members; and in 11 years, it grew to over 200 members. In the ninth year, New Life moved from a leased shopping center space into a purchased church property. God gave New Life a vision, a mission, and ministries that continue to reach the next generation for Jesus Christ.

In 2009, I was invited to serve at the national level of The United Methodist Church and subsequently moved to Nashville, Tennessee, where I served as a new-church strategist for three years. In 2012, I was promoted to the position of associate general secretary, New Church Starts Division, and executive director of Path1, New Church Starts of the General Board of Discipleship. My work included serving as chief visionary and advocate for creating "new places for new people" through new church plants and faith communities.

In 2014, I graduated from Wesley Theological Seminary with a doctorate of ministry degree in church leadership excellence. Additionally, I serve as a consultant, coach, and resource person to bishops, conference developers, and church planters in the areas of planting and sustaining new churches. My current position as a district superintendent for the Gulf Central area of the Florida Annual Conference started in 2016 and includes serving as the district's chief missional strategist.

The Gulf Central District includes 3.4 million people and covers four counties. There are 89 United Methodist churches in the district that has been entrusted to my oversight. My passion for effective church leadership continues.

I am burdened by the knowledge that existing black United Methodist churches (and others outside the denomination) are experiencing decline and difficulty creating and sustaining relevant ministries. This book serves as a resource for the church. I appreciate the opportunity to share my love of and appreciation for the black church that nurtured me and continues to do so today. I hope as you read this resource that you are reminded of wonderful personal experiences of being nurtured and strengthened by pastors, leaders, and members of black churches around the world.

Rodney

Although my family's spiritual roots are in the Church of God and the Baptist church, it was an invitation from young adults at A. P. Shaw United Methodist Church in southeast Washington, DC, that led me into a real relationship with Jesus Christ. A. P. Shaw was known as "Holy Ghost Headquarters." It was a vibrant multigenerational church with several choirs, dynamic worship, ministries for all ages, and a culture of evangelistic outreach that was second to none. Nurtured in this vibrant spiritual environment, upon graduation from high school, I joined the United States Air Force.

My years of military service afforded me the opportunity to grow spiritually while on active duty. I sang in the choir, served as a liturgist, and eventually preached my first sermon in a military chapel under the encouragement of the base chaplain. Although I was assigned to several different duty stations, I was never far from a chapel; and God sent laity and clergy alike to encourage me to pursue my call into ordained ministry.

After completing associate and bachelor of science degrees, I left the Air Force and enrolled at Gammon Theological Seminary, Interdenominational Center in Atlanta, Georgia. The first six months of seminary, I attended Douglasville United Methodist Church, where Pastor O. B. Davis generously opened his pulpit to young preachers. Pastor Davis invited me to serve as a student minister. Six months later, I was appointed as a student pastor at the Marietta United Methodist Church in Cedartown, Georgia. During that two-year period, the congregation grew. We began the construction of a church parsonage, and I moved from a student appointment to a full-time appointment.

The day I graduated from seminary, I found out that I was being appointed to a new church start in southwest Atlanta. That new church became Hoosier Memorial United Methodist Church, and the membership grew from 18 members to over 600 in four years. Many of the principles that led to that congregation's rapid growth are found in this publication. The numeric increase opened doors for me to consult with other congregations in the areas of congregational development and evangelism.

My next appointment was as director of evangelism and revitalization ministries at the General Board of Discipleship in Nashville, Tennessee. I later returned to Atlanta to serve for ten years as senior pastor of historic Central United Methodist Church. Working together, the church grew numerically, new ministries were launched, and a 2.7-million-dollar educational facility was built. During this time, I also completed my doctorate of ministry degree and served as an adjunct faculty member of the Interdenominational Theological Center, teaching church administration, evangelism, and worship courses.

My next appointment was to Ousley United Methodist Church in Lithonia, Georgia, where I served as the first African American pastor. Located in a growing area of suburban Atlanta, the congregation increased rapidly and became a vital place of worship.

In June 2001, Bishop Felton May asked me to return to the Baltimore–Washington Conference to attempt to save a congregation that was struggling after the departure of its senior pastor from the church and the denomination. The church was in debt and was a mere remnant of once having been one of the largest churches in the conference.

Despite our best efforts, this bold experience of survival ended with the disbanding of the congregation. Realizing that the congregation was unlikely to survive long-term, a new church-start—Covenant Point United Methodist Church—was launched. Many departing members of the disbanded congregation joined me in creating a new and vibrant worship community.

I was later asked by the bishop to move to First United Methodist Church, Hyattsville, Maryland, a large, dynamic, multicultural congregation. This church provided me with a clear picture of what a congregation made up of people from diverse cultures has the potential to become in a diverse and complex society.

Upon his arrival as a new bishop, John Schol invited me to serve as director of congregational development and as a guide for the Baltimore–Washington Conference. The guiding ministry gave me the opportunity to serve as a resource for several congregations.

I returned to the pastorate to serve St. Paul United Methodist Church in Oxon Hill, Maryland. During that six-year tenure, we formed a cooperative parish with a predominantly Anglo congregation, Corkran Memorial United Methodist Church. Our partnership with them continued until they grew strong enough to operate once again on their own. During this same period, the St. Paul family paid off the mortgage on the sanctuary and office facilities.

During this season, I continued consultation services for other churches and served as a coach for several pastors and local congregations. As a coach, I began seeing the importance of creating systems that would provide long-term vitality to congregations.

My next appointment was to a cross-racial setting. I once again found myself as the first African American pastor of an Anglo congregation, Liberty Grove United Methodist Church in Burtonsville, Maryland, a suburban community of Washington, DC. Currently, I am now back on the annual conference staff, serving as Director of Leadership and Congregational Development for the Baltimore-Washington Conference.

Lessons I learned in small towns, urban settings, multicultural cities, and suburban areas, combined with 37 years of service as a congregational consultant and leadership coach are incorporated in the pages of this book. And while this publication focuses on the black church, fundamentally principles for congregational vitality are universal. Application of these principles is most effective when applied contextually. It is certainly true that culture is more important than strategy. This publication offers years of proven strategy; but, more importantly, this resource offers a pathway to interpret culture as the transformative agent that creates vital emerging black churches: resurgence.

Together, through this resource, Candace and I hope to share our personal leadership experiences at the many levels of the church where we have served. While neither this or any other publication can be all things to all people, we are sharing information about practices and strategies that are indeed working in a number of places. This is not so much a "how to" book as it is a book of shared experiences that have resulted in positive and measurable ministry results.

As lifelong learners and leaders, we bring to this publication different gifts. But while our experiences vary, our commitment to sharing these experiences as teaching tools is focused on collaborative learning as a clear path to effective leadership.

Conclusion

Resurgence in ministry flows from the deep wells of proven principles and strategies learned and perfected in the trenches of ministry. There is no *Ministries for Dummies* book that automatically makes a minister effective. Experiences, good and bad, shape life-giving moments that when reflected upon in the context of culture, experience and learned wisdom, create successful ministry. This resource, therefore, is a conversation about proven methods that when applied in a ministry setting where people are genuinely interested, produce positive results.

Reflect and Respond

1. Create a list of ten past, present, and future opportunities for your ministry. Determine which item is a landmark or part of the emerging landscape.

2. Name at least five landmark scenarios within your ministry setting.

3. Name at least five landscape opportunities within your ministry context and community.

4. Which do you tend to focus on: the landmarks or the landscape of ministry? Can you see both?

5. How adaptable are you to the changes that we discussed earlier in this chapter?

6. As a leader, what is the one thing that you are passionate about as it relates to your church and community?

7. As a leader, where do you invest your time and resources in the hope of making ministry better for the people you serve?

8. What makes the hearts of your congregation sing? Worship? service to the community? leading new believers to Christ?

Action Items:

1. *Innovation* is a word that is often associated with industry and not ministry. But in the context of this resource, it is used to mean the opportunities and God-blessed moments when in cooperation with the leading of the Holy Spirit, God gives us that unction of the Spirit to improvise, improve, and innovate something that will radically transform the way we do ministry. We believe that God-inspired innovation leads to transformation.

2. In Isaiah 43:19, the prophet Isaiah instructs the children of Israel not to "remember the former things nor consider the things of old for God is about to do a 'new thing' now it shall spring forth, shall you not know it or perceive it?" God is always innovating and inviting us to join Him in the "new things" He is doing and wants to do in the midst of our ministry settings. Our work is to "perceive" it.

CHAPTER 1

From the Industrial Age to the Digital, Downloadable-on-Demand Age

"Every once in a while a revolutionary product comes along that changes everything." – Steve Jobs

What does an instant camera, a VHS tape, a cassette tape, and a brick-and-mortar bookstore all have in common with a smartphone? Nothing—and everything all at the same time! Fifteen years ago, these were all viable million-dollar industries that delivered specifically unique services to consumers.

Back then, I (Candace) bought books and magazines at Borders and then went to Blockbuster to rent movies on VHS. I listened to music and messages on my handheld cassette player. If I wanted to take pictures and see them instantly, I would grab my Polaroid instant camera, load the film, and point and shoot. The quality of the picture was OK, but I didn't have much else to compare it to as it related to instant photos.

Today, most of these production industries have experienced revolutionary changes in their businesses, if they have not already gone out of business, sold off assets, and laid off employees. But have we stopped engaging in using the Industrial Age services they offered?

In the current digital, downloadable-on-demand age, these services are delivered on one handheld device: a smartphone. A phone can serve as a movie or publishing distributor as a video store or a bookstore would. It has a camera ten times better than the old instant cameras, and it has replaced the cassette tape and tape player as a device for enjoying music and messages. Think about how seamlessly we've accepted and integrated our phones into our lives.

Central United Methodist Church, Atlanta, Georgia

In my (Rodney) years serving at Central United Methodist Church, it was customary for members to dress in hats and suits on Sunday morning before heading to church, where they would receive a paper Order of Service. Once the service began, someone would stand to give the weekly announcements, the congregation would sing songs from hymnals, and then the Word would be preached.

Each Sunday had a theme. First Sunday included Communion service, with hymns and anthems sung. Second Sunday was filled with blended anthems, spirituals, and gospel songs. Third Sunday, the children and youth choir sang; and Fourth Sunday, the gospel choir sang.

On average, the worship service lasted two hours, often taking the form of a celebratory revival-like worship, political rally, community workshop, and prayer service; and then there was the financial appeal. After the service ended, people lingered another 30 minutes or so for fellowship because gathering and being part of the church was the heart of the community and the main source of information and connection.

But today we can connect with people via social media throughout the week and hear their joys and concerns. We can like their posts and the pictures they share. We can contribute to the church whenever we think about it by going to the church's website or app to give online. We can read the church announcements on the website and listen to a sermon we missed on the church's podcast or online archive.

We still want to come to church and worship God corporately and fellowship with other believers, but we appreciate the shorter worship services because we also have lunch plans, sports activities, kids' activities, and/or work social activities on Sundays now. So we appreciate a church that also offers earlier or later worship services to fit our busy schedules. And instead of the hats and formal suits and dresses we used to wear to church, casual clothing is the preference for many on Sundays. Some of us wonder why people even bother to dress up anymore.

Welcome to the "digital age" requests and demands of people considering attending your church. Is your church acknowledging and finding ways to address and adapt to these requests and demands? Are there areas in which your church still invests primarily in methods of the Industrial Age instead of connecting with people by using tools of today's digital, downloadable-on-demand age?

The message of the good news of God's love through Jesus Christ is unchanging, and people still need to hear and receive this message. But the methods used to share and communicate this message have changed, and the world has moved through the Industrial Age into the digital, downloadable-on-demand age. This chapter will challenge and invite leaders to discover and engage new digital, downloadable-on-demand resources in a current and future ministry context.

The Black Church Shaped by the Industrial Age

The Industrial Age was shaped by industry, production, and productivity. From the steel mills of Pittsburg to the car manufacturers in Detroit, to the orange groves and orange juice plants of Florida, every company produced high volumes of goods. During the Industrial Age, America was a place of industry; and entire communities, including churches, were built around these industries. Managers were rewarded for employee productivity; and employees were rewarded for producing and following plans and doing their part to contribute to the whole of the process.

But we must ask ourselves, *How was the black church (pastors, leaders, and members) part of the Industrial Age workforce influence as we think about churches of that time?* Whether we had professional, manufacturing, or service industry jobs such as teachers, nurses, secretaries, housekeepers, porters, butlers, maids, longshoremen, drivers, or general laborers, the Industrial Age influenced the black church. While highly valued as employees in certain industries, we also saw these same characteristics appear in church programming and structure.

As part of the black church, we further explored the example of organizational identity. This was especially evident when people made new acquaintances.

After being introduced, if a person wanted to know more about someone, he or she would usually ask, "What church do you belong to?" A typical response might be, "I'm a member of Mt. Calvary, where Rev. So-and-So is my pastor." Adding church identity as part of shared information gave people a sense of the community to which they were connected. If they talked more, they would then share what they did at their church, for example, choir member, usher, deacon, or missionary. These were communities that brought great pride, and identification was something received in exchange for faithful service to and for the church.

The Black Church Shaped by the Digital, Downloadable-on-Demand Age

The movie *Thank God It's Friday* hit theaters in 1978. It told the story of people who regularly enjoyed singing and dancing at a particular disco. Donna Summer sang the theme song, "Thank God It's Friday, Friday, Friday." I (Candace) was ten years old and remember hearing the song on the radio. The song was so popular that it helped coin the acronym TGIF; and later the TGIF restaurant chain opened, a place synonymous with good food and good times.

Fast-forward 30-plus years, and mention TGIF to young adults today. More than likely, their definition of *TGIF* is probably tied somehow to social media. Same acronym but—in light of the shifts in industry and culture brought on by the digital, social media, social network age—it now has different meanings to different people in different generations.

As we think about this illustration and the black church, think about ways the digital, downloadable-on-demand age has, and is, shaping the church today. One of the first lectures I heard that described the influence and the impact of the digital age and the opportunity it presents to the church was by Leonard Sweet, theologian and professor of evangelism at Drew Theological Seminary in Madison, New Jersey. He used the acronym EPIC to start a conversation about ways the church could create EPIC experiences:

- Experiential
- Participatory
- Image-Rich
- Connected

What does it mean to create a worship service that is experiential, participatory, image-rich, and connected? These are questions that the digital age invites us to ask as we plan worship services.

There are several well-known large membership black churches in The United Methodist Church: Windsor Village and St. John's, Houston, Texas; Impact Church, East Point, Georgia; and Ben Hill Church and Cascade Church, Atlanta, Georgia. These churches, while different, possess the following similar traits:

- They are served by dynamic pastoral leaders.
- They attract a large number of diverse and middle-class members.
- They have diverse ministries.

Many people overlook the fact that all of these ministries began as new-church starts, church revitalization projects, or small-membership churches. They were led into vibrant ministry by the effective implementation of strategies that caused them to grow beyond a small-membership mentality. The resulting growth is now history.

Some said that we would never see that type of significant growth in black churches again, but Impact Church and St. James have proven that statement wrong. At the time of this writing, *Outreach Magazine* recognizes Impact Church as the 59th fastest growing church in America. And St. James continues to grow in Alpharetta, a northern suburb of Atlanta. This resource captures some of the best things that result in effective church growth and vitality. These churches are also examples of resurgence in local churches that continue to evolve in their leadership, worship experiences, and ministries to meet the needs of multi-generations in the digital age.

Resurgence celebrates the past but is also focused on emerging principles and practices that direct the path of ministry into creative and innovative strategies for the future. Let's explore the ways your church can use the current digital technology available in your ministry context.

Digital, Downloadable-on-Demand Ministry Strategies

People use many digital and social platforms in our society, but your church should not feel pressured to engage all the platforms. Instead, find the best one that members of your church are already using.

Survey the congregation, and ask whether they use any of the current social media platforms. Your church can create a communications team (digital ministry team) of volunteers that is knowledgeable and understands the power of media as a significant ingredient in ministry and missional outreach.

Social media today is what the printing press was in the past. Churches that do not invest in digital media are signaling that they do not intend to invest in a vital future. Social media presence is a must for churches to engage in resurgence.

Evangelism Through Technology

Many churches are using technology as a platform for evangelism. Robust websites have morphed from simply being single-page websites to being more informational, inspirational, and interactive points of entry for many churches. These platforms extend the outreach of ministries beyond the Sunday morning worship experience. Church on Sunday is no longer a single day of events because social media has extended the worship experience far beyond just Sunday morning.

A question we ask consistently in this resource is, "Who will do this with us?" For answers, we asked millennial social media strategist L.K. Rich to collaborate with us. She designs and runs social media campaigns for churches, for profit ministries business, and not-for-profit organizations; and she was excited to contribute the content and strategies for the rest of this chapter.

Through technology and social media, churches now have the opportunity to share the "personality" of their church, or the manifested body of the church, with more people. Whereas, traditionally, people who wanted to get to know a church better would have to visit a service, today they often go online to become better acquainted with a church before they ever walk through the doors. They are looking for what the church does and says outside of Sunday morning; and they are looking to see what that church does in its community and how it addresses the issues of the day, the tragedies of the moment, the currents of change, and the rifts within society.

Keeping that in mind when telling stories or writing captions or copy for your websites or various social media platforms, it's important to filter all that you share through the following questions, paired with your church's mission statement (who/what your church says it does or is). Adding your mission statement to the filter of questions helps to keep your church body's voice consistent.

- How does this connect or reflect our mission?
- How are God's arms reaching?
- How are God's hands healing?
- How are God's words teaching?
- How are God's feet going?
- How is God's love showing them there is a way?

Content Creation Is All About Relationship

We researched a local church whose adapted mission statement was "Committed to guiding people to Jesus through the salvation of Jesus Christ." That's a pretty lofty mission statement!

As a social media team, we begin by asking, "How do we create content that resonates and relates not only to our church but also to the ever-evolving communities in which we currently abide?" But when we drilled down through the filtering questions to discover the answers, we found that it becomes content that resonates and relates.

The latest incident affecting our community is the killing of an unarmed black man. So if our mission is to be committed to guiding people to Jesus through salvation of Jesus Christ, *how does what happened connect or reflect our mission?* It connects and reflects our mission because right now our community is grieving the loss of persons and personhood, and it's questioning our humanity in a state that has objectified us instead of seeing us. Through this incident, we have to help our community experience the love that carried Jesus to the cross.

How are God's arms reaching? To further connect with our communities, will we post on our website and other social media outlets and extend invitations for people to come together to grieve and experience Jesus' love shared through His people?

How are God's hands healing? Will we touch the community through outreach promoted on our website or plan to attend a vigil or a march as a church?

How are God's words teaching? What about Jesus's salvation story can we educate in an editable yet not oversimplified way to help guide us and root us in the likeness of Christ as we search for answers, justice, and understanding?

How are God's feet going? As we share and write about going to the altar, where else might our feet take us to be among the people and offer them the heart of Christ?

How is God's love showing them there is a way? As we face this most recent death, will we demonstrate to our communities that they are loved and can find support from their church family? Instead of teaching "respectability politics," will we celebrate and highlight that people in our communities are loved and worthy of love just as Jesus displayed during His own diminishing experiences in society?

After identifying these filters, we now have a variety of options to create content using technology or other church offerings that represent engagement in the community and care outside of the church walls and Sunday service.

It is important that the church body's voice should be magnified in all website and social posts, not just in the voice of the person who is responsible for posting or the pastor of your church. Unless your pastor is a nationally recognized televangelist-type person, most people won't have the connection that you do with him or her. Being mindful of this will keep your social media posts a reflection of the whole body and its role in the larger community instead of just one person.

It's okay to post quotes or writings that your pastor may want to share, but do so from the standpoint of it being good information and not from the perspective of "our pastor says." You may not hear it like this, but think of the person who is simply looking for God's love to show them a way to make it through their current reality. How does that person hear it?

Technological evangelism isn't a stretch, but again it sounds lofty. This type of outreach is more than simply posting a daily devotion or an inspirational quote. Technological evangelism is reaching out to people with the intent of working through the different filters that make up your church's manifested voice. It clearly shows who your church is and what your church is about.

The final things to consider are technical and important components in creating content that generates engagement.

- *Use clean images that are in focused, solid composition and feature stellar lighting.* Your phone's camera will work as a great starter tool.
- *Post succinctly, using few words on images and in captions.* Say what you need to say, knowing people read things when they are succinct, visually pleasing, and to the point.
- *Be consistent in posting.* Uniformity of your posts across all platforms, including your website, is critical.

Church Social Media Strategies

Social media strategies are not one-size-fits-all, just as church ministries and missions are not the same across churches. To assume that I could tell you the best strategy for your church would be imposing on your church and your churches resources.

Three things are key to cultivating a strong social media strategy: (1) Discover your "why," (2) develop consistency, and (3) connect with the platform that the majority of your people use. Many social media strategists suggest that you have a presence on all platforms. But if you find yourself in a situation with minimal resources and time, it's important to pick the platform where your people are and where you'll get the most engagement.

Monitor your engagement on social media. It's wise to heavily monitor your social media and respond with the voice of the church and the heart of God to people who may comment. This might mean you have to delete obscure commenter posts or fake stories with addresses to send money for a sick family member.

Stay up to date on existing and new social media platforms. Another wise thing to do is to take classes, research information, or hire a social media strategist. (If you're interested in finding a social media strategist, search LinkedIn or use the recommendation of a trusted person who may know a strategist with demonstrated know-how, proven results, and an understanding of the church context, and who has a solid work history.) Taking classes, researching information, or hiring someone can help you identify the "why" of starting the church's social media account and what your posts outside of inspirational quotes, church announcements, service time, and devotionals will convey. The content filter questions will also help you create a unified voice for the content you post.

Educating yourself or hiring competent help will assist you in better understanding the different platforms and how to use them. Most of the more popular platforms have a live component, and all of them have an algorithm that affects the way your content is shown and found.

Understanding this information will help fine-tune a strategy that fits your church and your church resources. A clear social media plan will help you enlist volunteers, which can serve on various teams to get your strategy off the ground.

Online Worship Services and Giving

Online worship services are a must for today's culture. There are congregants who are sick or homebound, or they may be out of town or have an unconventional work schedule. So being able to connect or to stay connected with the church as a remote member is a real phenomenon in the way churches are tracking attendance and "doing church" today.

Watching a livestream of the service and being able to give online are important to vital congregations now and in the future. The online service and giving options eliminate any barriers that traditionally may have prevented congregants from experiencing a church service due to life circumstances.

And today church members are experiencing the ease of giving through various programs and apps. Each of them has its own price and fees that apply.

These options of worship and giving don't take away from the traditional sacredness of the sanctuary, of worship, and of the offering plate. Instead, they make the worship and giving experience even more tangible wherever a congregant may be, locally or globally. In this way, congregants are always connected to their home church literally and monetarily, which hasn't always been the case in the past.

Using Technology for Church Meetings

Using technology to facilitate routine committee meetings or high-level check-ins is not only a great way to be an effective steward of time through maximized efficiency, but in some cases, it can also keep an entire committee or auxiliary on the same page. Whether you meet in person and use technology or meet virtually, there are various resources available to make your meetings happen seamlessly. For example, Google Docs/Basecamp can be used as a planning center to store committee notes and create a six-month meeting calendar, with alerts and reminders of upcoming meetings.

Virtual meetings are so readily available that even parents who travel can use technology to say goodnight to their children. And many virtual "face time" technologies exist to make connecting with others easier.

Stay abreast of the latest technology that can help you reach your audience. Constantly evolving services are out there, and using search engines or talking to your tech-savvy neighbor will often reveal the latest tech invention to meet your needs.

Online Small-Group, Christian Education, and Mission Opportunities

In expanding our in-person congregational communities to online communities, understanding the place of online small groups, Christian education, and mission opportunities can be difficult. Each of these areas seem to naturally fall under this umbrella because they appear to be connectional opportunities that would be better done in person.

But people are currently searching online for ways to meet other people off-line, face to face, to connect with and forge lasting relationships. So even though they may use social media or small-group and Christian education opportunities similar to online learning to connect with like-minded people, they will inevitably migrate from online to in-person and create lasting connections built on the basis of life similarities.

When people are interested in missions, they search for and join Facebook groups for mission and service opportunities that resonate with their core values of wanting to give back. These same groups are meeting in person and committing to mission as a way of building connections and friendships, while helping or aiding their fellow man outside of natural disasters and tragedies.

People look online to find a church's small groups, Christian education opportunities, and lists of missional engagements. In doing so, the objective is to find and engage with like-minded people, hoping not only to connect with them but also to build lifelong connections through practicing life together as an extended family.

As you begin navigating resurgence from the Industrial Age to the digital, downloadable-on-demand age, the strategies discussed in this chapter will be helpful. We are available to assist you in connecting with excellent coaches, professional social media strategists, and resource people to help your church in effectively using social media and digital and technological resources to enhance your ministry.

Conclusion

Every church will not grow into one of the fastest growing churches in America. The focus of this work specifically targets churches that were once vital but now find themselves engaged in ministry in a tough place, struggling to survive. Churches that live into the principles and strategies that are offered in this resource can once again become vital places of ministry.

Reflect and Respond

How will you navigate?

Consider these five strategies, and apply them in your current and future ministry:

1. Know your audience and your current and future ministry context. Then shape the worship experience to meet the needs of the overall audience.

2. Resist the temptation to shape the worship experience solely on a past Industrial Age model and the interests of power brokers in the church.

3. Discover ways to incorporate digital, download-able-on-demand experiences in current and future worship experiences.

4. Acknowledge those whom you are not connecting with, losing, not reaching, or disregarding by not navigating the shift in the current and future ministry landscape.

5. Acknowledge those who might consider your current worship experiences outdated because they see no signs of the modern digital age incorporated into the worship experience.

Action Item: The word *navigate* is a verb that means "to steer a course through a medium." Navigation is the science of getting ships from place to place. In this resource, we are inviting leaders to engage in the science and art of navigating as leaders called to lead the church from its current known place into the future God has in store for the church in our post-Christian culture and pluralistic society.

Today, navigation for the church leader is not a "maybe so"; it is an "absolutely so." Navigation is the fruit of embarking upon uncharted waters with a specific destination in mind. In the church, that destination is discerned and influenced by God's vision, spiritually connected leadership, resources, and the wisdom of a team of advisors who seek and sense the need for mid-course corrections along the journey.

As you navigate from the Industrial Age to and through the digital, technology age, know that the ministry terrain is changing so quickly that vital organizations often contract coaches and consultants to regularly review and tweak their ministry plans as they seek innovative approaches to expand their ministry focus. If you are a denominational member, check your conference for available staff to consult with you to help assess your church's health. They can also resource your church in the area of technology. This can occur one-on-one or through group coaching experiences.

Resurgence consists of constant mid-course corrections fueled by new information gained from informed opportunities to improve our destination. To have a vital church, have someone with outside eyes examine the systems of your church to ensure that systems and strategies are evolving in proportion to the church's growth goals.

CHAPTER 2

From Egypt to Canaan: Navigating Generational, Historical, Cultural Values and Differences in the Black Church

"There is an occasion for everything, and a time for every activity under heaven." – Ecclesiastes 3:1 (NIV)

Today, many historic, traditional black churches have memberships spanning the five generations known as Silents, Builders, Baby Boomers, Gen-Xer's, and Millenials. Each generation brings with it different values, leadership styles, and life experiences. A multigenerational leadership framework can help churches move through conflicts and navigate toward progress in the context of current and future ministry.

We started this chapter by framing it first as a conversation about generations. We wanted to highlight the values of the different generations and add to the Strauss and Howe generational conversation the framing added by colleague Dr. F. Douglas Powe from his book *New Wine, New Wineskins.*

Generation name	Birth years Ages in 2012	% of total adult population*	% of Internet-using population*
Millennials	Born 1977–1992 Ages 20–35	30	35
Gen X	Born 1965–1976 Ages 36–47	19	21
Younger Boomers	Born 1955–1964 Ages 48–57	20	20
Older Boomers	Born 1946–1954 Ages 58–66	14	13
Silent Generation	Born 1937–1945 Ages 67–75	7	5
G.I. Generation	Born before 1936 Age 76+	9	3

*Source: Pew Research Center's Internet & American Life Project, April 29–May 30, 2010, Tracking Survey. N=2,252 adults 18 and older.

Civil Rights Generation: 1921–1940
Black Consciousness Generation: 1941–1960
Integrationalist Generation: 1961–1980
Hip Hop Generation: 1981–2000

Powe refers to the Civil Rights Generation as including persons born between 1921 and 1940. Well-known people from this generation include Martin Luther King Jr., Malcolm X, Maya Angelou, and Diane Dash. The Civil Rights Generation is also known as the Change-Agent Generation. They organized to enact changes that are still embedded within American culture. This generation worked to endow African Americans with freedom and dignity. In fact, Powe describes this generation as valuing freedom and dignity for all people. And they challenged others to reinterpret the understanding of the American dream.[4]

---

4 *New Wine, New Wineskins: How African American Congregations Can Reach New Generations,* by F. Douglas Powe (Abingdon Press, 2012); pages 8–11.

Powe further describes the Black Consciousness Generation. The people of this generation were born between 1941 and 1960. People of the Black Consciousness Generation include Jeremiah Wright, H. Rapp Brown, Jessie Jackson, and Angela Davis.[5] This generation built off of the Civil Rights Generation by emphasizing the beauty of blackness. The shift went from a strong emphasis on interracial cooperation to black empowerment. They deepened the understanding of the systemic nature of social ills.

Powe also describes the Intergrationist Generation as people born between 1961 and 1980. We are reminded of how this generation made history with the election of the first African American president, Barack Obama. Powe names this generation as "opportunistic because it inherited a legacy from the two previous generations that allowed for social, educational, political and religious mobility not typically afforded to previous African Americans."[6] Notables of this generation include Tupac, Jill Scott, and Erykah Badu.

Powe points out that lifestyle afforded to and experienced by many of this generation to some degree fractured the African American community, creating a divide between those who "got out" and those who still live in predominantly depressed African American communities.[7] Upwardly mobile African Americans started driving back into the neighborhoods they previously left in order to attend church, but many of these individuals lost all connection with the community outside of the church. With the mobility of this generation, we saw a significant shift in the view of the black church as the center of the community. I can identify with Powe's description as I am part of this generation and started a new church toward the end of the 1990s.

5 Ibid
6 Ibid
7 Ibid

Powe describes leaders from the 1990s as the Hip-Hop Generation. They were born between the years 1981 and 2000.[8] Famous people from this generation include Beyoncé, Serena and Venus Williams, LeBron James, and Raven Symoné. Powe describes this generation as highly valuing capitalism. They focus on the economic side of the American dream. This generation is fascinating in the way it has continued to shift the social, educational, political, and religious landscape for African Americans. The generation Powe calls the Hip Hop generation are also known as Millennials.

Black Millennials and the Black Church

Dr. Joshua Mitchell has written an excellent book called *Black Millennials & the Church*, which can help us understand young adults born between 1982–2000. Currently, Millennials represent the largest generational group in US history. This generation has grown up with technology, gaming consoles, computers, and smartphones and are known as digital natives. However, this generation is underrepresented in many of our black churches today.

According to a study by the Pew Research Center, 19 percent of blacks under 30 are unaffiliated with a religion, compared with just seven percent of blacks aged 65 and older. Mitchell says, "Black Millennials are increasingly disinterested in traditional church experiences. Despite our best programming and outreach efforts many churches have been unable to attract, retain and spiritually develop a substantial number of this generation."

A tangible way that Mitchell recommends a church can intentionally engage Millennials is to think through how to give them access to the content we want to share with them. But we must understand that as digital natives, this generation can use their phones to watch videos, order groceries, purchase tickets, conduct banking, and call or

---

8 Ibid

text someone at their convenience. As the church seeks to connect and continue to build relationships with young adults, be aware that the church can take the first step in making adjustments to reach and engage them. We will continue the conversation about how the black church's resurgence can intentionally engage black Millennials throughout this book.

From Egypt to Canaan

As the content and context of this chapter continued to unfold, we thought about framing it from "old school" to "new school," looking at generational differences and leadership dynamics in the black church. But that seemed like an oversimplification of what was becoming a complex, layered conversation, especially as we started thinking about current examples of black churches that we currently coach and consult. We reflected on the entrenched challenges many are facing and how the different values of the leaders, based on their generation, are factoring into their position and perspective as they wrestle with the future of their respective churches.

We landed on "From Egypt to Canaan" when Dr. Smothers was reminded of a chapter in *Singing the Lord's Song in a Strange Land* by Rev. Dr. Joseph E. Lowery. In Chapter Six, "It's Time to Move to Another Mountain," we found the Scripture "You have skirted this mountain long enough; turn northward" (Deuteronomy 2:3) to be a verse that spoke to both of us about the shift that is happening in the black church and the time to move and experience a resurgence.

Many historic, traditional black churches that experienced a heyday of sorts during the height of the Industrial Age and the pre- and post-Civil Rights Movement are finding within their current ministry context an aging membership, buildings in need of repair, a shift in focus from ministry to maintenance, financial challenges, an internal focus, and neighborhood gentrification. Churches facing these challenges are in need of and can experience resurgence!

In this chapter, we will discuss some of the perspectives, mindsets, and factors that create this convergence. We will offer resources to assist you in successfully navigating through this ministry context and into the future.

Here's what's being faced by many historical, traditional black churches in need of resurgence:

- Remembering that at one time this was "the church," but it's now stuck because it stopped reaching beyond its past.
- Discovering that if faced with the decision to relinquish the building and relocate due to gentrification or demographic changes, it is important that the conversation be framed in a way that honors and hears the various perspectives of each generation while it discerns the best decision for the current and future ministries of the church.
- Having the ability to understand how each generation presents views and how each values the current church location and future church location.
- Engaging members in conversation regarding "Big Mama's pew" and traditions like "selling dinners" that enabled the church to be where it is today.
- Struggling with how to honor the rich history, traditions, and institutions that were started from this church.
- Determining what is at stake if we move or what will happen if we don't move.
- Acknowledging if the perspective of some leaders is "what we were is bigger than who we can

become," while also acknowledging the fear of the future and how it is influencing perspectives. (We will later address how you can give place to fear as part of the "grief process" of churches in this stage of the church lifecycle.)

- Reflecting on the church's history and historical significance in the Industrial Age and pre-/post-Civil Rights ages. Then reflecting on all that has changed in the church as a result of the current digital, down- loadable-on-demand age. Reflecting about the potential relevancy the church can have into the future.

Recently I (Candace) led a workshop discussing the realities of how the black church has transitioned over a 200-year period in the United States. The following chart summarizes a high-level, broad perspective that also helps frame this conversation. The negro church emerged from slavery throughout the Reconstruction period, and it can be estimated that it emerged around 1790 and transitioned during the 1930s.

As the needs and consciousness of black people began to awaken, the black church was born. The black church began in the 1930s and continued through the 1990s. We are not saying the black church has ended, is dead, or is not relevant. We are acknowledging that over the last 20 years we have been in the midst of an evolving black church.

The traditional mainline black church has been impacted by the megachurch, prosperity gospel, rise of nondenominationalism, multicultural churches, and new churches. There are also people making the decision that they do not want to go to church at all. We affectionately call this group the "nones" and "dones."

The 200+ year journey of the Black UMC Church in America

The Black Experience in America	A Relevant Black Church emerged to address and support the people living into these realities	Context of the Mission Field in which the church existed
Pre & post slavery, negroes migrate, start schools, free men & women start creating strong families, communities, identity & church is central... while Jim Crow laws prevail, industrial age	The Negro Church 1790 – 1930's	
Black people make progress despite segregation. Blacks see their power to fight against unfair employment, education, housing civil rights & church is Central to community.	The Black Church 1930's – 1990's	
Multigenerational, digital & technological age, hip hop generation, dis-integrated black community, suburban living, mass incarceration, poverty, crime, black families interests are many, church options are many, black UMC church declines unless it becomes more relevant	The Black Church for a New Millennium 1990's – present & future	

In this resource, we are seeking to name the current realities surrounding the traditional black church in 2018 and beyond. We are naming the realities not to frighten you but to help you address, engage, and navigate these new realities in an adaptive way and not just through temporary "technical" fixes. Even though it seems to have caught us off guard, God is on the journey with us, guiding us from Egypt into the Promised Land.

Then we turned around and went back into the wilderness following the route to the Red Sea, as God had instructed me. We worked our way in and around the hills of Seir for a long, long time. Then God said, "You've been going around in circles in these hills long enough; go north."
—Deuteronomy 2:2-6

God instructed Moses after some time of wandering in the wilderness that it was time to go north. Today, it's time for our churches to move in a new direction—the direction that God chooses to lead us into the future.

As you honestly assess the health of your church, consider whether you (the church) have been wandering around in circles: the same programs, music, meetings—just a different day or year. Are you ready to stop wandering in circles and go in a new direction?

When I (Rodney) was young, my family would often drive to Ohio to visit my oldest brother, who was in the Air Force. My Dad loved to drive at night, and my mother would ask me to be his co-pilot while she would dose off for a nap.

I loved taking the late night, early morning shift, particularly when we would drive through the fog in the mountains. I once asked Dad how he knew where to drive when the fog was so thick that he could barely see the road ahead. He replied, "When I can't see the road ahead, I just follow the white line in the road. As long as I can see the line on the road, I know that it will safely keep me in my lane and help me navigate the road." This resource has a similar purpose. It provides signs and signals that keep us on the road to revitalization.

As a pastor or a lay leader in your current church, if your leadership journey appears foggy at this time, know that you are not alone. As you seek to lead your church in resurgence, know that it might seem foggy now, but keep your eyes on God and on the road ahead. Keep leading into the future!

In the midst of conflict, we can look like a scene from *The Beverly Hillbillies,* a sitcom from the 1960s and 1970s. One episode involved Jed standing on the porch, not moving from his current spot, while Granny stands next to him holding a gun. Both are trying to maintain the status quo and guard their place only to discover they are standing on a gold mine (crude oil) that is about to create a different future for their family.

You will encounter resistance as you seek to lead resurgence, and that resistance is rooted in the comfort of staying where you are and not changing. Some people can be adamant in their resistance, and they might even dig their heels into the ground to avoid changing. In the case of Jed and Granny, they discovered they were standing on a fortune of "black gold"—oil. Once the oil was discovered, it was easy to move into the new places and new spaces the new resources afforded them, such as a mansion in Beverly Hills.

As you evaluate your church assets, you might also discover a "gold mine" that will resource your next season of ministry. In the face of resistance, we also have to remind ourselves that everyone didn't go into the Promised Land. Some stayed and even died in Egypt. As a leader, you can make it through the wilderness. God's promised land is just ahead of you.

Reset

When a personal computer (PC) gets stuck, freezes, or stops working, you can simultaneously hit the Control, Alt, and Delete keys to reset the computer. The Alt key is similar to the shift function. It's used when you want to modify to produce a different function.

Similarly, the good news for a church in conflict about its future is that it, too, can reset. It can start by pressing Control to relinquish and release control of the desired outcome wanted for the church. Then press Alt to shift and modify plans and processes. During this phase, it is important to avoid having "winners and losers" and "yes" or "no" voting as the decision-making framework. Instead, they should ask themselves what they need to Delete from their plan and process in order to welcome in God's Spirit to guide them toward experiencing resurgence in the context of present and future ministry.

Conclusion

What we've learned through each of the cycles of societal change is that the black church is a highly adaptive organization. Today, with the evolving social, cultural, technological, and ecclesiastical landscapes, we must constantly reassess the ways we do church in a society that does not necessarily value church as the priority it has been in prior generations.

At the heart of resurgence is understanding that the core purpose and message of the church does not change. The church exists to make disciples of Jesus Christ for the transformation of the world. The church can adapt our methodology and rebrand our message and activities in ways that offer relevance in the midst of a plethora of life choices today.

Since the church is no longer the center of life for some, we must create viable choices as an important institution providing those things that can only come from the church. They include transformational community, inspiration, collaboration with other community services, and centers of social change. More than just a place of worship on Sunday, the church must become a seven-day-a-week community resource center. Our ministries must translate into everyday life skills to equip people for vital purposeful living. Resurgence invites churches to discover God's expanding vision for creating new community from Sunday to Sunday.

Reflect and Respond

1. Pastoral leadership and the community surrounding the church have changed. Has the church lost its vision to make disciples? How have membership demographics and the surrounding community changed?

2. What happens when churches lose sight of their vision? What happens to a long-standing church that has had several pastors but no continuity of vision from the past to the present to the future?

3. How can we move through this fog and move through memorializing who we used to be and start creating a vision of who we can become?

4. Discover and create a vision of the future of the church that has continuity through the past and how church members see themselves involved.

5. Acknowledge and engage in the church grief process, including providing grief counselors as resource people. Entering the grief cycle helps place anger, denial, pain, blame, and guilt into perspective as you work through it and seek to come to a genuine place of acceptance to start the healing process. Place your hope and trust in God again for a future vision for the church that is greater than the past. When churches are enthralled and embroiled in grief, it's easy to lose sight of the "why" of us being a church today.

6. Rediscover and define the current and future "why" of being a church.

7. Remember the church's mission ultimately exists to make disciples of Jesus Christ for the transformation of the world.

8. Acknowledge all the other ways that black churches have contributed, shaped, and given opportunities for people of faith to grow and engage socially, politically, educationally, relationally, and spiritually.

Action Item: One of the foundational principles of resurgence is adaptability. God's emerging process must continuously be taught in our administrative meetings and from the pulpit. Change for the sake of change is not helpful, but change that increases cultural awareness and accessibility is necessary to attract and connect with emerging generations of church attendees.

Church meetings must evolve from being merely repair sessions into being strategic planning and execution gatherings. In other words, these times of gathering should present a well-planned agenda of two primary things: strategies for implementation of ongoing growth goals, and execution of ongoing projects and ministries that benefit the ministry and the community. Once again, the goal is to look ahead and prepare the ministry for current and future opportunities.

Meetings should be aimed toward actionable items. Lay leaders and clergy should come to the meeting prepared to present solutions and resources to implement goals that have already been determined. This approach changes the tone of the leadership team from "vision busters" to "vision implementers."

This change of leadership purpose takes place in three different ways. First, the structure of the leadership team should be reduced to a manageable size of 12 to 15 people. The single board model is a good example of how few people can accomplish great tasks in the life of a ministry.

Second, the composition of the leadership team should include people with skill set abilities to implement the future vision for the ministry—within and beyond the church doors. An outside consultant or coach can be used to assist the church in clarifying its emerging vision and purpose.

Third, the leadership team's task is to monitor and balance the traditional roles and functions of long-term members with the emerging vision. Rehearsing the past as important, but continuing to build on the past in order to accomplish new things accomplishes this. What you don't want to do is throw out the baby with the bath water!

When I (Rodney), introduced technology into Christian education classes, I started with a class for seniors on the use of computers, tablets, and mobile phones. I helped lower their resistance to use of these devices by showing them how the devices could be used to keep them in touch with their grandchildren. All change, especially change in the church, requires a hook to the past and a bridge to the future.

Updating church financial systems along with the use of kiosk and mobile payment systems will take slow deliberate introduction, instruction, and implementation. Children and youth are always helpful as ambassadors of change. They can assist the leadership team in providing communication platforms for easy use.

Our denomination is rich with training resources. Discipleship Ministries, UM Communications, UMC Mission (Global Ministries), Higher Education and Ministries,and other agencies in the church have great online resources that assist in telling the story of our past, our present, and our future.

CHAPTER 3

From the Civil Rights Era to the Black Lives Matter Movement

"But let justice roll down like waters, and righteousness like an ever-flowing stream." –Amos 5:4

Thoughtfully and prayerfully, read the scenarios—based on a true story—throughout this chapter. Then reflect on how your faith community might have responded in a similar situation and how that response could be improved to benefit the whole community.

Tragedy in the Streets

Sirens wailed and blue lights flashed. People were yelling and screaming. Across the street, crowds were gathering. A mother yelled, "My baby, my baby, what happened to my baby?" Someone shouted, "He was running, and I think the police shot him!" Cell phone cameras flashed while the EMTs attended to the wounded.

A 15-year old black male had been shot. Young people were outraged as yet another "one of us" had been shot for no apparent reason. This had to stop. Our lives matter! Black Lives Matter! "We 'bout to do something. We ain't just gonna sit around here and act like this is okay. 'Bout to get in these streets and make some noise, take some action."

Rev. Jones, who pastored the church across the street, spoke up in the midst of the crowd, "Can we all stop for a minute and say a prayer?"

It took a minute to quiet the crowd down. One young man said, "Y'all show the preacher some respect."

They settled down in respect for their fallen peer. The pastor prayed, "Heavenly Father, we come before You with bowed heads and humble hearts, seeking You for wisdom, guidance, and strength in the midst of this violence and police brutality on these streets and in our neighborhood. Be with young James as he goes to the hospital. Don't let him die, Jesus, but save his life. Guide the doctors as they treat him. Comfort his mother and friends at this time; and please, Jesus, give us wisdom on how to respond. Grant us your peace. It's in Jesus' name I pray. Amen."

After the prayer, a young man spoke up and said, "Okay, Rev, we prayed. What's next?"

The crowd looked on, awaiting Rev. Jones's response. The church members looked on from across the street, waiting for the pastor to return so the board meeting could start. The pastor internally was distressed and unsure, but he responded by saying, "Son, we have got to trust God."

The young man responded, "Rev, I don't mean you no disrespect, but we are trusting God, and we about to go down to this police station and protest until we find out why that cop shot our friend. 'Faith without works is dead,' right, Rev?" the young man said confidently. "We 'bout to put our faith to work!"

The crowd rapidly disbursed. The young people followed the young leader down to the police station. Some people just lingered.

Feeling uneasy, Rev. Jones returned to the church. The waiting members asked what happened. "Another shooting in our community, and it seems like the police were involved."

One church member said, "This community is so unsafe. These children are out of control, and the parents don't know how to parent. I just don't feel comfortable in this neighborhood at night anymore."

"Can we start the meeting already?" said another church member.

The pastor sat silently through the meeting, wondering about the young man's condition at the hospital, hoping he survived, wondering how the victim's family was coping as they sat waiting for word on his condition. He wondered if they needed anything. The pastor's mind was miles away from the board meeting.

"Reverend, are you going to vote on this issue?" the deacon asked.

"I abstain." Rev. Jones grabbed his bag and excused himself from the meeting. He admitted to himself that he didn't know what to do, but he courageously asked the Holy Spirit to guide him to do something.

What should be his next step? Would he go to the hospital and offer pastoral care to the family? Would he join the young people at the police station? Would he go home to the suburbs and complain to his colleagues about the violence that exists in the neighborhood that he is called to pastor? What would he do? What should he do? Can this black church experience resurgence?

The Black Church and the Fight for Justice for All

The black church and its leaders historically have been part of the fight for justice and equality in communities in this country. We can continue to engage in opportunities within our communities to help dismantle the negative "isms" of today and work together to create a more just and generous society.

Historically, the black church has played a significant role in fighting for and advocating for justice and equality.

- Faith has been vital in shaping the progress and journey of blacks in America.
- The church helped shape black dignity and culture.

- The church has provided leadership, identity, and social significance for black people.
- The black preacher has typically been one of the best educated in our communities, a person of scholarship and spirituality.
- The church was at the forefront in advocating changes to laws that created injustices toward black people in their churches and communities.

Navigating Blacks Moving to the Eastside

In the 1960s and early 1970s, changes in the Civil Rights Act, Voting Rights Act, and Fair Housing Act opened up new opportunities for black people. The television sitcom *The Jeffersons* referred to this phenomenon as "finally [getting] a piece of the pie." This phenomenon created significant shifts in black communities, churches, and black people overall.

As blacks migrated to the suburbs and began to have access to previously denied jobs and housing, we began to see the creation of a black middle class. These shifts were significant in large Southern cities like Atlanta, Dallas, and Houston. "White flight" from the suburbs created opportunities for blacks to move to suburban neighborhoods and gain access to abandoned churches, which were previously home to white congregations. In The United Methodist Church context, churches like Ben Hill and Cascade grew to become two early megachurches in metro Atlanta, with weekly worship attendance exceeding over 1,000 people.

In his groundbreaking book *Disintegration,* Pulitzer-Prize winning columnist Eugene Robinson describes this growth and class phenomenon in the African American community. Robinson defines these four classes of blacks as (1) Transcendent, (2) Mainstream, (3) Abandoned, and (4) Emergent.

These class distinctions in the historical and traditional black church shift focus away from justice to a salvation message that was more about personal salvation and sanctification and less about corporate, collective, and community salvation and community transformation. Since the early 1980s up to the present, we have watched and experienced many black churches move their focus exclusively to issues such as personal and spiritual growth, along with the rise of nondenominational, Word, and prosperity gospel churches.

This expression and shift of focus of black churches created the perfect storm, as the values, needs, and emphasis of mainstream blacks differed significantly from the class of people still living in urban cores and inner cities. The social economic gaps continued to grow throughout the 1980s and 1990s and into the 21st century.

Fast forward to the digital age, and we begin to be aware of the rising number of incidents of police brutality against young black males. These types of incidents didn't just start happening in the digital age. But today, more people have more access to technology to record what has been taking place; whereas in years past, the media had exclusive access to such technology and could determine what they were going to broadcast. Phones with cameras and voice recorders have enabled virtually everyone on the street to become an investigative reporter.

In addition to wrestling with the impact on the black community of joblessness, homelessness, sexism, racism, and discrimination against LGBTQ rights, almost weekly, we see the rise of police brutality. In response to this rise, three courageous young women created the Twitter hashtag #BlackLivesMatter. Indeed, black lives do matter, and young people are protesting in the streets of Ferguson, Baltimore, Chicago, New York, Los Angeles, Nashville, Atlanta, Minneapolis, Baton Rouge, Dallas, and other cities.

What is the church's response? Where is the traditional black church in light of all that's happening in communities today? Churches need to experience resurgence and once again engage around crisis and chaos facing communities experiencing police brutality, gun violence and other societal ills that include poverty, low-performing schools, joblessness, and homelessness.

Recent incidents of racism and alt-right protests and rallies by white supremacists have been discussed as the debate over removing Confederate statues continues. The Obama era has ended, and the Trump era has begun. This new era seemingly has brought with it more overt racism and incivility in our society than I (Candace) have experienced in my lifetime.

In many communities, it seems as if a number of traditional black churches are disconnected. Many have become like silos. We formed selves to serve selves to be about selves. But the emerging events on the horizon require us to get out of our buildings and find out what the community needs. We should never embrace the attitude that the church cannot help or make a difference. The church can make a difference, but it requires leaving our buildings, identifying community needs, and walking alongside others into their emerging future and preparing for what is to come. The early church was a primary incubator for equipping generations for success, and this mandate should be at the heart of resurgent church agendas.

By its nature, the church must see itself as systems within systems in order to provide care for entire communities. The church doesn't have to offer only spiritual help. It can offer spiritual empowerment that addresses the holistic needs of people in the community.

Unfortunately, many church leaders have not been trained in how to engage chaos and crisis. Instead, many have been trained to lead in times of comfort and care.

For a resurgent church to succeed, it will require leaders to be retrained. Usually, this type of training is not going to happen with church leaders going to a retreat or a seminar. It's most effective when church leaders go out into the community and engage the people and the real issues they face. When pastors and church leaders go into the community and get to know the people, they place themselves in an excellent position to invite the community into the church to engage in conversation on how the church can have a more positive impact in the community.

Where Do We Go From Here?

The day after James was shot in front of the church, Rev. Jones went to the monthly gathering of pastors and community leaders. At the meeting, he saw his colleague Rev. Denise Strickland.

Rev. Strickland is the senior pastor of a traditional church that also has a contemporary service with a hip-hop flavor. The church is in the same neighborhood where James was shot, but on a different street. Rev. Strickland is a recent seminary graduate and sees herself as a pastor in and with the community. By her own admission, though, she didn't start out as that type of pastoral leader.

She had to learn how to be a resurging leader. Trained in seminary to preach, administrate, and provide pastoral care for a black church, Rev. Strickland quickly discovered that the issues of the neighborhoods surrounding her church weren't covered in the seminary curriculum. Over time, she realized she had to make a choice. One option was to stay within the walls of the declining church, busying herself and the people with inward focused "church work." Another option was to "be the church—making disciples for the transformation of the world."

Deciding to be a disciple-making church, the members discovered ways to be the church serving beyond the walls and within the community. Asking God to open their eyes to see the needs beyond the church, Rev. Strickland and church leaders acknowledged the systemic poverty, joblessness, health and family issues, crime and violence, regentrification, and other issues happening within their zip code.

After studying *Walking With Nehemiah,* by author and community pastor Rev. Dr. Joseph Daniels, Rev. Strickland's church found ways to address the distress in and around their community. The pastor and some of the long-standing members started praying, asking God to open their eyes and hearts to what was happening in and around them. They prayed and asked God to help them be present in the lives of the people they were called to serve. And they asked God to resurge them so they could be part of God's plan for the rebuilding of this community.

The prophet Isaiah reminds us that God continues to call leaders to fast and pray, to become the advocates of justice and equity in response to the cries of the hurting and the oppressed in a way that honors God. Isaiah 58:11-12 says God will guide us continually and satisfy our soul in drought. We will be a watered garden whose waters never fail. The blessings of God are not just for us. God expects us to rebuild, restore, and repair. God wants to see our communities and the people residing in them repaired and restored. Who does God use to accomplish this purpose? God uses us.

A Church Experiencing Resurgence

One might say Rev. Strickland's church, an older black Methodist congregation, experienced a resurgence of sorts. One change over time as a result of their resurgence assessment, the help of a coach, and much prayer was the church vote to relinquish an entire worship experience to the Millennials that attend regularly.

The Millennial experience has its own liturgy, style, music, and message, along with service (ministry) and online giving opportunities. Some attendees worship at this location, and others do not. As Rev. Strickland stays connected with this part of the church body, she has discovered that even though some in this age group do not physically come to the church building regularly, they are still engaged in "being the church" in the community.

Outside of the church walls, these young adults meet, gather, fellowship, brunch, worship, pray, study Scripture, give, and serve. Rev. Strickland has had to learn how to pastor multiple congregations within one church and doing so is not without its challenges. Some of the older members would rather Rev. Strickland spend most of her time accommodating their spiritual and temporal needs while spending less time with the people "outside of the church."

Rev. Strickland admits that when she first arrived at the church, she was accommodating to the Civil Rights Generation, the older members of the congregation who represented consistency in membership and the bulk of church tithers. They paid her salary, and she liked the comforts of ministry. She also had enormous college and seminary debt that needed to be paid. She thought if she could keep this part of the church body satisfied, all would be well. She never anticipated feeling empty and unfilled in a ministry that was only inwardly focused.

One day, she noticed a gathering of young adults near the church. A few were church members she had not seen in a while. After engaging them in conversation, she learned why they were more comfortable outside the church than inside. Perplexed and unprepared, she engaged these young adults in conversation. She discovered some of what kept them disconnected from the church.

Over time Rev. Strickland trained and equipped more lay people to become involved in the caring and sharing ministries of the church. As a result, the older adults felt cared for, while the middle-aged and young adults were slowly starting to reconnect with the church as it created space for them to use their unique gifts and abilities.

Along this journey of resurgence, Rev. Strickland learned a valuable lesson: Attention to one (group) without attention to the other (group) hindered the vitality of the church in the community. But because of the church members' willingness to change and grow, the church is experiencing resurgence.

From Comfort Managers to Crisis Partners

Millennial leaders are not looking for black church pastors to come in and "manage" anything. Social media reports examples and new information from church pastors as they experience the crisis in every city that violence and police brutality is happening.

The crisis of our opening story started shortly after a young black man was shot by a white police officer. Some older black pastors entered the crisis with the assumption that their presence and authority would be accepted based on their titles, not on any previous relational capital they had with young activists. Many of the pastors who had no such connection were "laughed to scorn" and were said to be out of touch. The activists asked, "Who are you? Why have you come? Why should we listen to you?"

The pastors were told to leave because they did not have implied or assumed authority just because they wear clergy collars and preach in protected Sunday space. Some of the pastors left and chose to write the activists off as thugs, but others decided to stay and humbly learn to lead as partners in the emerging movement.

When facing crisis, we can look in the pews and find numerous resources already available. We simply need to value, appreciate, and rally around what is already part of the fabric of our churches. Some people may get stuck at this point and say, "It's a problem," but there are many opportunities for the black church to emerge, even in crisis.

The first thing we need to do is see how we are equipped to engage the needs and opportunities at our doorsteps. The inability to equip congregations to engage crises is not as severe as we think it is. It's simply a matter of connecting call, spirituality, and commitment to Christ in a way that is not just limited to the Sunday morning experience but rather engages people between the Sundays. When people in community are struggling with racism, sexism, discrimination, addiction, unemployment, and violence, the church can no longer sit by, absent from the table when conversations about these issues are taking place.

In days gone by, we talked about being in the choir or being on the usher board. However, being in the choir or on the usher board may not be the answer to social issues communities face today. Resurging churches rally people to come up with solutions to community issues. The church resurging does not need to be on the periphery of social issues and change. Instead, the church can be at the heart of it all, but first we have to admit we can't do all of these things alone.

The black church must move intentionally from being impotent as a single force to normally and naturally envisioning community partnerships and coalitions so it is not overwhelmed. No one church can do all things; but when churches come together with one another and other entities in the community that can solve these problems, it becomes a powerful force for the Kingdom.

How do leaders address and respond to chaos and crisis effectively? There are seven "L's" that are instructive in helping us move forward.

- *Love all people.* We must begin loving all people. We must stop worrying about man-made labels and personal history and move toward developing genuine love for all people. Let's meet people where they are. We are called to love the Lord with all our heart, mind, and strength and love our neighbor as ourselves (Matthew 22:39).

- *Listen more, and talk less.* We must stop talking so much and start listening more. We must become better listeners in community. We have to hear what young people have to say. Contrary to popular belief, they are not all angry. They are not all disengaged. They have powerful words to communicate that need to be heard and considered. We are called to be quick to listen, slow to speak, and slow to get angry (James 1:19).

- *Learn from new places and new people.* We must learn from new places of education and inspiration. One size does not fit all. In this culture, we learn in many new ways. We now have more ways to receive information than ever before. There was a time when there were only three national television networks. Now we have hundreds of stations, instant streaming, and internet sources, which are primed to take us into a whole new dimension of learning, entertainment, and communications.

- *Live, lead, and be present in the now.* It is important that we live with current reality, not just talk against it or be afraid of it but live with it. Even though the past was glorious, it doesn't compare to the present and the great future God has in store for us. We are living in the times we are living in on purpose, not by accident. Let's ask God and trust Him to enable us to be relevant in the times we are living in today. "Don't remember the former things or consider the things of old for I am about to do a 'new thing' now it springs forth shall you not perceive it?" (Isaiah 43:18-19). Let's ask God to sharpen our perception and discernment.

- *Lead into the future.* Leading means taking on the feelings of hopelessness and powerlessness within our communities and addressing both with new perspectives. We may not be able to solve all of the issues our communities face; but with God's help, we can make substantial inroads toward positive change. Paul reminds us that we can forget those things that are behind us and press toward the future that is before us. We can press toward the mark of the prize of the high calling of God in Christ Jesus (Philippians 3:14-15).

- *Launch from a place that creates a win-win.* Everything that is a solution for the church does not have to start its conversation in the church. Believe it or not, there are people in our communities who are trying to build bridges to us and want to partner with us in many significant ways. Consider that churches generally take up one of the largest pieces of real estate in the community. And there are seniors, young people, and families looking for space where they can gather. Solution: The church. However, the typical traditional model has the church primarily energized one day of the week rather than every day of the week. In order to serve more effectively, the church must be in tune to community needs and open to partnering with the community to meet those needs. This launching also means that we move beyond the comfort of the pews and engage political, social, and financial systems to ensure that when we see problems such as immigration, discrimination, bullying, gang and gun violence, school shootings, police brutality, sexual harassment, #MeToo, human trafficking, and abuse, we are not complicit by not addressing them. Instead, the church becomes a powerful advocate in people's lives, working with other local powers and principalities to alleviate community problems.

- ***Learn and lead with others in addressing current justice issues.*** In 1966, Dr. Martin Luther King Jr. shared a lecture assembly in Hollywood, Florida, entitled "Don't Sleep Through the Revolution." He said that, unfortunately, people as well as organizations are in the midst of great change but miss the cues that should prompt them to get involved and be part of what's going on. The church doesn't have to be afraid of change. Instead, it can join with others so it can better address the issues in the community.

Micah 6:8 reminds us, "And what does the LORD require of you? To act justly and to love mercy and to walk humbly with your God." Jesus instructs the religious people in Matthew 23:23 and calls them hypocrites: "Woe to you, teachers of the law and Pharisees, you hypocrites! You give a tenth of your spices—mint, dill and cumin. But you have neglected the more important matters of the law—justice, mercy and faithfulness. You should have practiced the latter, without neglecting the former."

This was a tough word for me (Candace) to receive, but nonetheless true. I can easily neglect the importance of addressing justice issues because I'm so busy focusing on mercy ministries and ministries that strengthen people in being faithful Christians. Biblically, justice is standing up to the king or the nobles for the fair treatment of all people. Justice involves dealing with the systems that are at the root cause of the injustices in our communities. We all can learn and lead with others in addressing the systemic injustice issues facing people in the communities we are called to serve.

Recently, I joined the ecumenical organization FAST (Faith and Action, Strength Together) that seeks to address justice issues in Pinellas County, Florida. I appreciate being part of a group that works with church leaders to address issues around the need for civil citations for first-time youthful offenders. We recognize that black children are receiving a disproportionately high number of criminal records instead of civil citations. The need for affordable housing is another issue we are addressing together as churches show strength in numbers through partnership with this community organization.

Learn and Lead Together in Addressing Community Issues

Following the police shooting, area pastors called a community meeting that Rev. Jones and Rev. Strickland attended. Before the meeting began, the two pastors had a chance to talk to each other.

"Hey Rev, you heard about the shooting in front of our church yesterday?" Rev. Jones asked.

"It's the third shooting in a month, and this one involved the police. The young leaders who gathered at the police station last night are now demanding a hearing. They were texting me all night. Once I found out what happened, I went to the hospital to visit with the shooting victim's mother. It was a long night indeed," Rev. Strickland said. "What about you, Jones? This time, the shooting was in front of your church. I heard you showed up."

"Yeah, I did show up, and it was a rowdy group. I prayed with the young people that had gathered around. They seemed so angry, but they were respectful to me and at least allowed me to pray with and for them."

Rev. Strickland responded by shaking her head in affirmation. "It was good that you were there and prayed. So what did you do after you prayed?"

Rev. Jones said, "The crowd disbursed, and I went to my board meeting. I was already late."

"I understand," Denise said.

"God is good," Rev. Jones said as he looked around.

After an awkward silence, the two took their seats and the meeting was called to order. After about an hour of listening to the presenters, the attendees took a break. Rev. Jones and Rev. Strickland gravitated to each other once again.

Rev. Jones shook his head and said, "That shooting was alarming. After I went to the board meeting, even after I prayed, I still wondered had I—or had we—done enough. It's the one thought I have not been able to shake.

"In the 70s, I was on the front lines with other black leaders fighting for justice and equality. Today's issues—all the new technology and the lack of respect for pastors and the institution of the church—have me not wanting to participate. You're younger than I am, Pastor Denise, and you are right in the midst of what's happening. I'm proud of you."

Rev. Strickland appreciated Rev. Jones's honesty in admitting where his disconnect was with what was happening in the community surrounding the church.

"Thanks for being honest and owning your discomfort and why you're not engaged," Rev. Strickland said. "I recognize that it's time for us as leaders in the church to be honest and transparent about the ways the church has become inwardly focused and not seeking to understand and meet black Millennials where they find themselves. As we work to address racism outside of the church, it's time we deal with the sexism, discrimination, and patriarchy that exists inside the church as well. The #MeToo movement is also knocking on the doors of the black church, and it's time we open the doors and start honest conversations about this work as well."

"You're right. Times have changed, and a healthier leadership model is needed in the church. We need a model that acknowledges God has created us all as equals. I for one am grateful for how black women have supported the church and the fight for justice. I'm glad to see you leading the church at this time. Let's work together."

Rev. Strickland looked at Rev. Jones to see if he was being sincere or patronizing. She paused but chose to stay focused on being honest and empowered as she talked and hoped Rev. Jones's fruit would demonstrate his sincerity in the days ahead.

"Would you like to get to know some of the young leaders as potential partners in addressing the issues?" she asked.

"Those young people are my grandchildrens' age!" Rev. Jones exclaimed.

"Yes, they are, and they are well educated, well trained, and ready to lead. They are the Joshuas; and, Rev. Jones, you're like Moses. Yet Joshua can still benefit from Moses' wisdom if he's willing to share it and affirm it's Joshua on the front line of the battle today."

Pastor Jones paused and then thanked Pastor Strickland for her wisdom and invitation. "Yes, I would like to join you. Please let me know when the next meeting is. I'll be there."

Conclusion

This chapter concludes by inviting us to think about the encounter and conversation between Rev. Jones and Rev. Strickland. Which pastor's experience do you relate best to at this time in your ministry? Are you aware of the issues facing your community, and what is your level of participation and engagement?

Resurgence church leaders are aware that we were not trained to lead through the chaos and crisis we are living in and experiencing daily. The lack of preparation is balanced by a commitment to trust the spiritual practices of prayer, Scripture, listening, and reflection to center us as we seek to lead and engage our ministry context daily. We are called to be Davids and Esthers, being fearless and finding our own armor to face the Goliaths of our day. Just like God was with them, God is with us.

Reflect and Respond

1. What's the state of the community in which your church is located?

2. What is happening in and around your church zip code?

3. What are you doing to address the needs and the issues of your community?

4. Are you and your church leaders doing enough?

5. Are you ready to engage one of the "L's" to lead with the partners in your community?

Navigating Into the Future

Action Items: *Innovation* and *application* are two words that must be reintroduced in the church as God's normal developmental cycles of change and transition. Every aspect of society is evolving around us. A resurgent church faces the challenges of appearing relevant as it tackles the change that surrounds culture and context.

Changing culture even shapes fast-food restaurants. For example, Chik-fil-a has hospitality as its primary mission. They continue to update their stores to accommodate the evolving hospitality needs of their customers. Yes, they sell food; but they understand that if they don't attract people to their stores, no food will be sold.

The church often trails culture because we focus much of our energy on what has worked in the past rather than dedicating more of our time researching what vital and growing ministries are doing to stay relevant in changing times. Different worship hours, changing ministry models, more casual attire, and increasing demands for more tech use in worship are some of the ways churches are seeking to change with the emerging cultural habits of their present and perspective attendees. It's not only these obvious things that are changing but also how we connect and interact with our members and visitors.

A larger challenge awaits the local church as we are called on to intervene and resource changing societal issues developing in our communities due to changes in federal, state, and local politics. With the erosion of local social safety nets, the church once again has to resume its role as more than just a "preaching station" but as a mission and ministry resource center. This requires training and deploying volunteers (servant ministers) in increasing numbers. In order to do this, the church must partner with community support systems. Our mission is being changed by the changing needs in our communities.

Advocacy, emergency management, social services, family intervention, drug and alcohol counseling, domestic violence, financial counseling, immigration, racism, sexism, discrimination, homophobia, gang violence, unemployment, senior citizen care, child care, and affordable housing are just some of the issues around which the church will need to form partnerships to address. When a property becomes available in our community that can serve as an additional site for shared community-based ministry or our ministries are asked to partner to provide space for daycare, childcare, or senior care, these opportunities often require greater faith and new commitments to impact our communities in new ways. The lessons and opportunities remind us that vital ministry requires us to move beyond just Sunday morning worship to find ways to impact our community between the Sundays.

Often, our ministry of presence between the Sundays is our greatest inroad to long-term survival and vitality. The question that is essential to ask in order to expand our ministry focus is, "Who will do this with me?" Churches involved in resurgence are always looking for partnerships that enhance their overall effectiveness in the community. This requires an additional skill set on behalf of the leadership team. The pastor cannot do all these things alone. The pastor's primary role is to identify, recruit, cultivate, and mature spiritual leaders who see the larger vision for congregational and community development and mercy and justice ministries.

CHAPTER 4

From Caretaker to Catalyst Pastoral Leadership

"Care for the flock that God has entrusted to you. Watch over it will-ingly, not grudgingly—not for what you will get out of it, but because you are eager to serve God. Don't lord it over the people assigned to your care, but lead them by your own good example. And when the Great Shepherd appears, you will receive a crown of never-ending glory and honor." – 1 Peter 5:2-4 (NLT)

"I planted the seed, Apollos watered the plants, but God made you grow. It's not the one who plants or the one who waters who is at the center of this process but God, who makes things grow. Planting and watering are menial servant jobs at minimum wages. What makes them worth doing is the God we are serving.

You happen to be God's field in which we are working. Or, to put it another way, you are God's house." – 1 Corinthians 3:6-9 (MSG)

Mr. Geoffrey Heard, one of the many committed lay leaders in my ministry development, spoke a powerful word into my life when I (Rodney) served as the founding pastor of Hoosier Memorial United Methodist Church in Atlanta, Georgia. Brother Heard said, "Leadership is a function, not an office." He helped me integrate the disciplines of pastoral training into the needed skill set of working with the non-profit community sector. He taught me how to get out of the office and into the community.

City Councilman C. T. Martin taught me the importance of attending neighborhood planning units and city council meetings to see how grassroots organizing efforts move through the political system and become policy and resources. At first, I thought that these time-consuming meetings took away from my local church. However, as I grew to understand the system, I also discovered that these meetings had a direct benefit to my local congregation and its surrounding community.

The primary goals of resurgence are to broaden appeal beyond the doors of the local church and to view the church as an integral community partner. While there has been a great deal of energy given to separating key institutions within the community, the resurgent church asks the question, "Who will do this with me?"

In this chapter, we will discuss the shift from pastoral leadership primarily focused on being a caretaker to pastoral leadership that is a catalyst for change in the church and the community.

Pastor as Caretaker

The caretaker pastor's primary role was to care for the flock and therefore focus on the people within the church walls. Preaching, teaching Sunday school, counseling, conducting meetings, and visiting the sick were seen as the pastor's primary responsibilities.

The seminary model of shepherding was wrapped around a strong belief that taking care of the flock was the primary task of the pastor. Reporting to a church office and working within that space from early morning to late evening, with people coming in and out, was considered the norm for most pastors. They focused on caring for what already existed with the unspoken expectation that they, in return, would be cared for by the congregation.

Positive Pastor as Caretaker Scenarios:

- When a congregation needs intentional healing from ongoing or unresolved conflict.
- When there has been pastoral or leadership misconduct, misappropriation, or mismanagement.
- When there is a need to rebuild trust.
- When a church has experienced a destabilizing event or issue and is in need of caring, consistent, and steady leadership to become strong and healthy again.
- When it's time to prepare the church for radical change.

Restrictive Pastor as Caretaker Scenarios:

- When a church is internally focused instead of being internally and externally focused.
- When a pastor acknowledges a natural giftedness to deeply care for people and doesn't take responsibility to ensure other important pastoral leadership functions are covered in the congregation.
- When a pastor needs to feel needed and be needed by the congregation so he or she focuses only on caring for members, avoiding and procrastinating the need to focus on other issues occurring in the congregation.
- When a pastor likes being liked and pleasing to people in the congregation, so he or she focuses primary attention on caring for certain segments of the congregation, caring deeply for some while neglecting others.
- When a pastor cares for people as a default because he or she is not able to admit having limited skills and preparedness to engage the complexities and challenges facing a congregation today and into the future.

The Move From Caretaker Pastor to Catalyst Leader

In the move from caretaker to catalyst, it is imperative that pastors network with leaders from other skill sets and disciplines. While the model of pastor as CEO became an extreme example of the migration from caretaker to catalyst, healthier models of intentional leadership that combine the call of ministry with the disciplines of servant leadership and empowerment change how church leaders lead.

Being invited to become a member of Leadership Atlanta, serving on community boards, and hanging out with other community leaders enhanced my (Rodney) perspective on leadership. The need for intentional leadership in the black church today requires strong skills in visioning, creating, organizing, and motivating the church and the community to action. For resurgence to occur, pastoral leadership must be focused on God's preferred future constantly being voiced to create emerging opportunities within the congregation and through collaboration with partners in the community.

Resurgence occurs when the pastor is present as a strong persuasive voice at the decision-making tables in the church and in the community. Galvanizing partnerships with educational, medical, socioeconomic, communication, law enforcement, and governmental entities is the model of a catalytic pastor.

The Move From Caretaking, New Church Pastor to Meeting With Catalytic Pastors and Leaders

In 1996, I (Candace) was 29 years old and was appointed to start a new United Methodist church in Jacksonville, Florida. When I moved to Jacksonville, I only knew two people in the city, and neither of them decided to join the church, so we indeed started from scratch. As I visited area United Methodist churches and nondenominational churches, several people I met encouraged me to meet

Pastor Vaughn McLaughlin, the founding pastor of The Potter's House Christian Fellowship. At the time, its membership exceeded 2,000 people.

Our new church start was going to be contemporary, and we were in the process of building out almost 10,000 square feet of worship space. The challenge with the build-out was the current architectural drawing had the church in a traditional layout with structural poles obstructing the pulpit area. The drawing distressed me when I saw it, but I didn't have experience with commercial build-outs, so I felt stuck in how to communicate my concern with the architect. Upon the encouragement of Elaine Kyle, who had joined our core team, I spoke with Pastor McLaughlin.

After attending a Friday Night Live service at The Potter's House, Elaine introduced me to Pastor McLaughlin as a new young pastor in the city. He and his wife, Lady Narlene McLaughlin, talked with me for over an hour about Jacksonville and engaged me in the new church plans. I took a risk and shared my dilemma with the current architectural drawings that I had brought with me.

Pastor McLaughlin asked to see them. After looking them over, he took out a piece of paper and redrew the plans to create theatre-style seating, which absorbed the poles, and replaced the traditional worship seating that had a long center aisle. It was a catalytic leadership moment. I took the revised drawing to the architect, who then redesigned the space. When others who had worshiped at The Potter's House visited our space, they remarked that it felt like The Potter's House. I agreed because Pastor McLaughlin had offered to help me.

Pastor McLaughlin held a weekly pastors meeting for multidenominational, multiethnic senior pastors. The group met on Wednesdays from 10 a.m. to noon, followed by lunch. The purpose of the weekly gathering was to provide leadership training, teaching, and fellowship. Participants were able to ask Pastor McLaughlin questions and glean from his wisdom. After all, he served as pastor of one of the fastest growing, innovative, contemporary nondenominational churches in our city!

Pastor McLaughlin invited me to join the weekly fellowship. Initially, I was intimidated, being the only female pastor in an all-male clergy group. While confident God had called me to pastor, I chose not to attend gatherings where I would be referred to by male clergy and female church members as "Sister Lewis" or not acknowledged as a senior pastor. But I learned I could work through my feelings of intimidation with this group of catalytic pastors who sincerely welcomed me and made space for my questions and perspective.

It took me two years to get comfortable in the group, and I admit I needed and benefitted from meeting with these catalytic pastors. When I finally admitted that I needed to be part of this group and could become comfortable in this space, for the next ten years, I attended whenever I was in town. I grew exponentially and learned from Pastor McLaughlin and the others. Almost 20 years later, the group still meets on Wednesdays from 10 a.m. to noon. I attend in person whenever I'm in the city, and I can join it now by live stream when I'm out of town.

Is there a group of catalytic pastors or leaders gathering regularly in your city that you can join?

An example of catalytic leadership and a community partnership approach that comes to mind is from my (Rodney's) tenure at Central United Methodist Church in Atlanta. The first was a ministry to senior adults called Reaching Out to Senior Adults (ROSA). A seminary student, Normal Phillips, started the project, and it focused on linking seniors in need with community resources that provided medical care, as well as nutrition and transportation services. Rev. Phillips galvanized several churches to take ownership of ROSA, and it became an important link in the safety and survival of senior adults in the church and the surrounding community.

A second example of the catalytic approach resulted in several churches combining resources to build houses in the Vine City neighborhood of Atlanta. Monthly pastor's meetings became a governing board that created networks, structure, and partnerships to provide affordable housing to low-income residents.

A third model of catalytic leadership was the Youth Enrichment Program (YEP). It was the shared vision of a young minister, Dr. Fred D. Smith, who led the Community Ministry Program at Wesley Seminary, and a young Grady Hospital physician, Dr. Jerome Taylor. This ministry galvanized clergy, laity, and community stakeholders to provide transformational teaching, community building, and life-skills training. Resurgence impacts ministries that empower people inside and outside the doors of the church.

Caretaker	Catalyst
maintains the status quo	challenges the status quo
doesn't see the need for a new vision	casts a new vision
avoids conflict	addresses conflict
peacekeeper	exhibits courageous leadership
Passive reforming leadership style	strategic and executing leadership style

Conclusion

Leadership is not about perfection. It's often about a vision that is shared, cast, open to feedback, improved, and iterated. For example, Apple has proven success in upgrading the iPhone's system, seeking feedback from its users, and developing new apps to improve functionality and performance. Similarly, discovering the unique catalysts that move your ministry forward is a combination of meeting felt needs and creating new opportunities for your ministry to become the answer for questions not yet asked.

Reflect and Respond

1. How do you understand your call as a leader in the black church today? How does it differ from how black leaders have historically understood the call to ministry and leadership in the church?

2. Instead of just taking care of what is currently happening, what does it mean to lead and create resurgence in this season of church life?

3. The question "Who will do this with me?" should be a normal part of any ministry effort that we undertake. The church as an island in community is an obsolete model. Enter partnerships with other community stakeholders. We must be pro-active in social activities taking place in our community. As you think about this statement, list names of new people you will begin to invite to join you in mission and ministry!

4. As you think about your primary pastoral leadership style, are you more of a caretaker, a catalyst, or somewhere in between?

5. In what ways can you identify potential partnerships with resources beyond the local church that will benefit your ongoing ministry efforts?

6. How can outsiders use your church facility as a source of revenue and a place of gathering for other community events?

7. How can your church partner with other ministries in your ministry area for the benefit of the community?

Action Items: Part of effective leadership is influence. Building relationships with other leaders in the community is a vital resource for collaboration and consultation. Think team, think community, think partnerships, think we.

Include community partners in your planning process. Also include them in your budget allocations. Invite members of the community to serve on ministry and planning units in your local church where appropriate. No longer can our ministries "plan for them"; we must include "them" (the community) in all of our planning.

Resurgence requires that we see ourselves as one of several stakeholders in the community. Our physical, financial, spiritual, and leadership assets should be offered to make our communities healthier and whole.

One of our greatest assets should be our influence because we have built relationships with our schools, neighbors, government officials, and other faith communities. Our mission and outreach should be intentionally geared toward creating these partnerships.

CHAPTER 5

From Boss to Teaming Leaders

"But each of us was given grace according to the measure of Christ's gift. Therefore, it is said, 'When he ascended on high he made captivity itself a captive; he gave gifts to his people.' (When it says, 'He ascended,' what does it mean but that he had also descended into the lower parts of the earth? He who descended is the same one who ascended far above all the heavens, so that he might fill all things.) The gifts he gave were that some would be apostles, some prophets, some evangelists, some pastors and teachers, to equip the saints for the work of ministry, for building up the body of Christ, until all of us come to the unity of the faith and of the knowledge of the Son of God, to maturity, to the measure of the full stature of Christ."
– Ephesians 4:7-13 (NRSV)

As the black church evolves, grows, and understands itself in relationship to the people that attend and the community and context in which it finds itself, the role of pastor and church leader continues to evolve. "Take thou authority" is what the bishop said to me when he laid his hands on my head and ordained me to serve as a United Methodist pastor. What I (Rodney) thought he said was, "You now have this expensive education, and you are charged to go and tell the people how to be the church." His instruction, coupled with a traditional seminary education, left me with the impression that I was the "expert" on all things "church."

Vital church leaders know that this model is not a preferred model of leadership.

This chapter will discuss the shift from a pastoral and lay leadership model of being and seeing yourself as the boss who tells everyone what to do, when to do it, and how to do it because you are the pastor a.k.a. The Boss. Today's ministry context invites pastors to shift and adapt and adopt a model of pastoral and church leadership that leads, equips, develops, and disciples people. The pastor as a leader of teams in no way diminishes the authority of the pastoral office, but it allows the pastor to serve in his or her strengths, inviting others to do the same.

A resurgence pastor is one who leads and builds teams of disciples to lead and serve in mission and ministry with their families, in the church, in the community, and throughout the world.

Where did the model of pastor as boss emerge?

- Historically, the pastor was the single leader and head of the church.
- In terms of education and training, the pastor was one of the most educated in the congregation.
- In terms of social authority, congregations gave trust and authority to preachers.

During the Industrial Age, the typical church model resembled a workforce with a boss and subordinates. The boss told everyone what to do, and people followed instructions and did their part in the widget-making process. In return, the boss paid each worker a fair wage. In the pastor-as-boss model, the pastor publically praises the contributions of the subordinates.

Today, the shift in culture no longer makes this the best model. People are more educated today, with varied experiences. Additionally, people can be relied upon to do their part in light of the multidimensional aspects of church and the multiple disciplines in which people serve and contribute outside of church.

Limitations of Pastor-as-Boss Model

- Limited scope of depth of perspective around what present and future ministry can become when it's limited to only what the boss can see.
- Does not allow the pastor to be honest about personal limitations of leadership.
- Creates unhealthy self-reliance on the pastor and does not empower the people to serve in their God-given gifts.

Moving Away from Pastor-as-Boss to Teaming Pastoral Leadership

As a new church planter and founding pastor, it was easy to see myself (Candace) as pastor and boss. When the church started, there was no one else but me as the planter. I was in charge. As people joined the new church team, I welcomed them. Since many had never been in church leadership before and I was the founding pastor, they assumed that I knew what to do.

Do you see a pattern here?

I've always had a healthy understanding of the Scripture that instructs us that Jesus is the head of the church, and I've always valued the phrase "we are the body of Christ."

"He is the head of the body, the church, who is the beginning, the one who is firstborn from among the dead so that he might occupy the first place in everything."
– Colossians 1:18 (CEB)

"You are the body of Christ and parts of each other."
– 1 Corinthians 12:27 (CEB)

I, like Moses, had a hard time delegating and sharing ministry responsibilities with others. But I'm grateful for the Jethros who assisted me in developing a team approach to ministry leadership. Jethro's assessment after observing Moses' leadership approach was recorded in Exodus 18.

> You will end up totally wearing yourself out, both you and these people who are with you. The work is too difficult for you. You can't do it alone. Now listen to me and let me give you some advice. And may God be with you! Your role should be to repre-sent the people before God. You should bring their disputes before God yourself. Explain the regula-tions and instructions to them. Let them know the way they are supposed to go and the things they are supposed to do. But you should also look among all the people for capable persons who respect God. They should be trustworthy and not corrupt. Set these persons over the people as officers of groups of thousands, hundreds, fifties, and tens. Let them sit as judges for the people at all times. They should bring every major dispute to you, but they should decide all of the minor cases themselves. This will be much easier for you, and they will share your load. (Exodus 18:18-22, CEB)

Pastors and leaders who choose the boss approach often wear out, burn out, and become frustrated and distorted in their view of the church and God's people. It's not that peo-ple aren't willing to help; they might not have been asked or equipped to share the load. Investing time in coaching, resourcing, mentoring, and apprenticing people to share in leadership in the life of the church is always time well spent.

I grew personally through coaching, reading, asking questions, and just admitting I was tired. My thinking shifted from me as primarily the boss who had to know and do everything and instruct everyone in every task. God was faithful in sending skilled people to join our core team as we started this new church. I had to shift to equipping people. I invited them to join me in training and Bible studies, and I shared resources. This shift enabled me to stop doing everything myself and begin to, as some say, "stay in my lane." Doing so helped me to add value to the team as a visionary leader sharing the load with gifted leaders.

Resources that helped us shift to a team approach at the church plant included spiritual gifts testing and completing personality profiles to better understand our different gifts and how we could work together effectively. I served as pastor at New Life for 12 years, and I'm grateful for the leaders who served with me and shared the load. They gave endless hours and resources to building the body of Christ.

Changing the church model from that of boss to leadership team leader creates an atmosphere for working with others to accomplish many ministry tasks.

Pastor-as-Boss Model	Pastor-as-Team-Leader Model
views self as the expert	creates culture of leaders and thinkers
views self as having all the right answers	invites people together to collaborate on solutions
views self as the final authority on all matters	authority is valued alongside responsibility without the team leader pastor relinquishing authority. It is made clear what areas the pastor will have final authority over after receiving input from others.

Pastor-as-Boss Model (continued)	Pastor-as-Team-Leader Model (continued)
views self as set apart by God and having spiritual authority to guide all aspects of church life	views the team as gifted and called by God to serve together as co-laborers in ministry together
views self as the only one with experience	views the team as having the ability to consistently work together to accomplish a common goal

The Teaming Church, by Robert Crosby, is a good model for maturing the entire leadership team of the church. When lay and clergy leaders mature in their respective roles and relationships, the church takes on healthier decision-making processes, funding to support the ministry vision becomes easier, and spiritual and numerical growth take place.

Teaming results when intentional and ongoing teaching about spiritual gifts, shared commitments, and modeling effective team ministry take place. Over the years, the role of pastor has evolved. Historically, in the black church, the pastor was thought of as the primary leader in the community.

Today, the pastor is often one of many people who bring education and experience to ministry. More important is the notion that the new norm for leadership in the resurgence movement is a group of people who lead alongside the pastor to create a community of leaders. From the Old Testament model of Jethro informing Moses of the need to enlarge the role of his leadership team to the emerging model of shared leadership at every level in the contemporary church, persons with specific gifts and expertise are the valued intent for growing and vital ministry.

This model creates ownership and expectation of involvement of the laity at every level in church life. While the primary role of spiritual leadership cannot be farmed out, it can be expanded when we take the time to identify and equip non-clergy persons to share in leadership roles in the church. Teaming is about more than just roles and positions; it's about, as Jim Collins stated, "getting the right person in the right seat on the bus." Another benefit of teaming is that it breaks down the "silo effect" and creates opportunities for people to work in community to accomplish tasks.

Teaming Pastor Model Requirements

This model is transformational and is anchored in coaching. It requires:

- spiritual maturity on the part of the pastor and team members
- each team member to possess healthy self-esteem— must check the ego in at the door
- clear understanding of respective roles and responsibilities, along with trust of others
- accountability

Top-to-bottom leadership may on the surface look like it is a more efficient way of leading, but in the long term, it is not. Resurgence cannot occur until the laity and or members of the church take ownership of changes and challenges that accompany forward movement. This results when there is buy-in from all stakeholders. Creation of this type of partnership in leadership occurs when three primary things take place:

- strong biblical teaching on the priesthood of all believers
- clear and consistent teaching regarding the call and ministry of laity as significant ministry gifts in and of themselves

95

- intentional teaching on the importance of creation and deployment of effective ministry teams. Empowering ministry teaming also provides continuity when pastoral transitions occur.

The Importance of Ministry Teams in Church Resurgence

Navigating the move from boss to team leader model involves clarity of call, sound understanding of collaboration, and a willingness to trust others on the team. Because so much of what we do today involves multiple generations, we must be sensitive to how multiple generations can effectively work together.

Contrary to popular belief, Baby Boomers, Generation X, Millennials, and Generation Z can work well together as long as there is a clear understanding of expectations and objectives of ministry outcomes. This cross-generational work requires a strong focus on working as a team where each person makes a contribution. To work effectively, this approach must be highly relational and built on mutual respect and trust.

Shared responsibility and accountability are the principles that undergird a successful partnership in the teaming process. The more teams look like teams of equals rather than teams with layers and layers of higher-ups, the more successful they become. A foundational principle of resurgence is to create community that attracts people from all age groups. This happens best when mentoring and reverse mentoring is an ingredient in the leadership mix.

The goal of teaming is to provide ownership of the ministry task at every level of the organization. With every new generation comes fresh eyes to solve emerging issues. When the church values those fresh eyes as gifts for its future vitality, that's when the community will begin to intentionally cultivate leaders of all ages and from all stages of life. Creating a culture of shared wisdom involves moving away from a boss model of leadership and closer to a shared model with many gifted people contributing to the ministry conversation. Creating a culture of collaborative learners and workers further creates a model of shared wisdom and accountability.

Leadership is a team sport. Our historic church leadership models have pretty much been top-down. Today, because of the complexity of leading churches, the better leadership model involves development of a team of leaders, men and women who are gifted in various areas of leadership.

Moses learned this team approach for leadership from his father-in-law, Jethro. In Exodus 18:1-27, Jethro teaches Moses the importance of having a leadership mentor, the power of transparency, having the best interest of one's mentee in mind, investing in the lives of those who are being, and having a teachable spirit.

As we learn from the men and women successfully leading organizations within and beyond the church, and after casting the vision, the primary role of a successful leader is team development. Healthy organizations are moving to team leadership models where members of the team complement one another in leadership skills and abilities.

The amazing part of the story of Jethro and Moses is that Moses shared his mentoring experience with Joshua, who became a great leader as a result of Moses investing in him.

This shift in leadership priority reshapes the role of the lead pastor and enables him or her to focus on other areas that require primary attention. This teaming approach also creates a culture of learning, leading, and launching new organizational capabilities. The benefits of having an effective team of leaders are increased capacity for these leaders to focus on visioning and the supervision of key players in the ministry.

I (Rodney) learned during a building project at Central United Methodist Church that I did not have all the experience for the planning, fundraising, construction, and implementation stages of moving the project from vision to completion. Thank God that there were men and women within the congregation who had expertise in all of those areas. Their insight and wise counsel allowed for the successful completion of the project.

What projects are you working on? It may be a room renovation, an expansion of the parking lot, the installation of a new sound system, or the replacement of the carpet in the sanctuary. There are people in the pews with amazing skill sets. Plus, involving them is an excellent opportunity to develop new skills in up-and-coming leaders. Shared leadership in present and future projects builds ownership, collaborative buy-in, faithful stewardship, and pride in team accomplishments.

Creating teams with people outside the church is also important. Every ministry leader should ask, "Whom will this action benefit besides us?" Creating a culture of collaborative witness will ensure that the community sees the church as a vested partner in the community.

Another way for church leaders to gain experience is to serve on community boards and other places of influence. We should be planning to get out of our church offices and spend a greater portion of our ministry time serving the community. Remember, leadership is a function, not just an office.

Younger leaders and leaders who are young at heart can intentionally create ministry models around equipping laity and other clergy for teaming ministry. The benefits are numerous, including creation of future leaders, seeding possibilities for multi-site ministries, and cultivating an environment of accountability.

Accountability is a valuable asset for being an effective leader. Without it, ministry can easily go off the rails, driven by self-centered, ego-driven personalities who think they know it all and can do it all.

By now you should be hearing our continuous theme of acquiring skill sets in community asset mapping, financial literacy, community development, leadership development, and other skills that can become vital ministry tools in the life of our local churches. But there is more.

Teaming ministries are great models for Kingdom expansion with proven, God-centered best practices that can be replicated in multiple locations. Teaming ministry becomes an in-house pipeline for developing experienced leaders. As our current shortage of younger clergy and young adults in leadership positions in the church occurs, teaming ministry becomes a great way to prepare these persons for future key leadership roles.

Other benefits to teaming ministry are the gifts, insights, and perspectives others bring to the table. Good ideas grow into great ideas; and when owned by a team, the likelihood of successful implementation of the ideas is significantly increased.

Remember, there is no *I* in *team*:

- There is exponential potential in the concept of "We/Team."
- In navigating the tough stressors of coaching, initially, it will seem easier to do it yourself than to go through the process of coaching someone else on how to successfully accomplish the tasks.
- Avoid jealousy, envy, and self-protection. Each can sabotage this shift, especially as you start seeing how God has uniquely gifted others.

Conclusion

Developing ministry teams begins with assessing the mission and vision of the local church and then building a team of people to move that vision and mission into execution of ideas and tasks. A teams' primary role is execution. It is organized to get things done. While it is true that leaders guide the "why" and the "how" of the forward movement of the ministry, the "who" is essential in execution of the pastor's vision for the future. That's the role of ministry teams.

In new models of ministry teams, development is an essential skill set. It is about development of leadership at all levels of the ministry and with essential partners beyond members of the church. Discovery of shared interests, collaborative benefits, and joint interest create a new leadership culture that incorporates the forming of crucial alignments. Collaborative planning, shared use of resources, and intentional team efforts expand the involvement position of the church to become a vital partner in the transformation of the local community.

Reflect and Respond

1. What is your current approach to ministry leadership? Are you a boss or a team leader? What supports your primary leadership model?

2. Do you have a Jethro in your life as you lead and serve in ministry? Why or why not?

3. How are you being mentored? How are you mentoring others to lead in ministry?

4. Who are you investing in for the future? In what ways are you creating a culture of empowering and equipping others?

5. What ministry area could use a team? Where will you begin building a new or strengthening an exisitng ministry team?

Action Item: Who Will Do This With Me?

The time when the solo pastor effectively handles every ministry need is behind us. A pastor's first question must be, "Who will do this with me?" The traditional model of the pastor being the sole source for all wisdom has evolved to a place where a wise pastor's first thoughts are now focused on getting the best people on his or her team. Resurgent pastors understand that success is found in the partnership of team and talent.

There is a cultural move toward storytelling as a way of assisting people in understanding how they are important to the ongoing development of an organization. Storytelling changes the narrative from seeming to be an expert on something to coaching others in building personal knowledge, skills, and experience.

Visiting ministries that are vital and growing become the best incubators of learning. Being able to observe and follow leaders as they go about their daily routines and then providing a context for questions and reflection provide an environment where the student learns best through observed behavior with the benefit of context and experience.

One of the reasons I (Rodney) am a big believer in seminary students being assigned as student interns is so that they can do ministry and then learn by doing the tasks for themselves. Allowing interns to lead various ministry functions provides them hands-on skills assessment, confidence-building experience, and a training environment where their real-life experiences are enhanced with feedback and reflections from more mature leaders. This approach also creates a normal team environment of teaching students how to work as part of a team.

CHAPTER 6

From Telling to Coaching Leaders

" They committed themselves to the teaching of the apostles, the life together, the common meal, and the prayers. Everyone around was in awe—all those wonders and signs done through the apostles! And all the believers lived in a wonderful harmony, holding every-thing in common. They sold whatever they owned and pooled their resources so that each person's need was met. They followed a daily discipline of worship in the Temple followed by meals at home, every meal a celebration, exuberant and joyful, as they praised God. People in general liked what they saw. Every day their num-ber grew as God added those who were saved."
– Acts 2:42-47 (MSG)

While in seminary, I (Rodney) had the opportunity to assist Dr. Melva Wilson Costen with her worship class-es. While doing my doctoral work, she allowed me to teach her courses while she was on sabbatical. That led to oppor-tunities for me to teach church administration. Dr. Costen coached me to the next level of my unrealized skill set that manifested into my becoming an adjunct faculty member. Dr. Costen didn't just tell me what to do and what not to do; she saw my potential as a future leader and coached me and created space for my teaching gifts to flourish.

In Chapter 5, we discussed the shift from boss to team leader. Bosses spend a great deal of time telling people what to do. A team leader spends time coaching and giving people opportunities and responsibilities, enabling them to grow to their next level of potential.

This chapter will focus on the pastor and leaders shift from telling to coaching. Coaching is key to resurgence because it creates new leaders who will help to expand our ministry impact.

Telling Versus Coaching

When you primarily view yourself as the pastor who is the boss, it's easy for you to see yourself telling others what to do. But the big picture and current landscape invites us as black church leaders to learn how to coach people and to invite them to become part of God's work in the world today. The church leaders who tell everyone what to do often feel the pressure of having to be at all meetings at all times because they've bought into the perspective that the people need them constantly to tell them what to do.

A resurgent leader understands the long-term benefit of knowing that God has given gifts to everyone and is committed to doing the work of equipping, releasing, trusting, and holding people accountable for the work of ministry that God has entrusted to our care.

Telling	Coaching
dispenses information	creates strategy
gives a plan	allows the plan to develop through conversations, feedback, and input from the team
focuses on events	creates systems to get things done
tends to be inflexible because it's his or her plan, not a shared vision	ability to adapt and adjust the plan with ease, then implement and execute it
limited by his or her own capacity	open to exponential growth and capacity based on shared ideas of the team

Releasing the Old Way of Telling and Learning a New Way of Coaching

Hanging out with more experienced pastors helps you learn life lessons that books can't teach you. Their wisdom about how to motivate and encourage members to move to the next level of ministry comes in understanding trust, momentum, and confidence in the pastoral and lay leadership.

It's not that vital congregations have had it easy. Each of them has experienced seasons of challenge. What is common to the congregations that are now thriving is that they trusted God for a new season of resurgence.

There is no magic pill that solves all church problems. What does create resurgence is a strategy that allows ministries to relinquish old habits and systems in favor of adopting new disciplines and systems.

The good news is that you don't have to figure out these solutions alone. There are now a variety of resources available, including written material, workshops, podcasts, and coaching resources that can come alongside your ministry to assist you in developing new and productive strategies to bring resurgence to your ministry.

Coaching bears fruit in many ministry settings. It allows an experienced leader to come alongside your leaders and assist them to craft the correct strategy to improve your ministry, equip your leaders, and to empower your laity to experience resurgence in your ministry setting. Coaching is one of the best investments you will ever make for yourself and your ministry.

Coaching is not a one-size-fits-all solution. What great coaching does is provide good assessment, resourcing, encouragement, and feedback. These combined elements result in new outcomes for your ministry.

What are the areas where you can benefit from coaching to improve your leadership skills in ministry?

One of my (Rodney) personal mantras is "New Thoughts, New Disciplines, and New Behaviors." Positive change and growth occurs in ministry because there is a commitment to evaluate the present and improve the future. Ministry growth in staffing, buildings, expansion of outreach, and greater mission involvement must all flow from intentional and prayerful goals to increase the impact of the ministry for its members and its community.

Holy Spirit-inspired and Holy Spirit-led motivation is the result of intentional prayer and programs, witness and work, and inspiration and intentional investment in the future. The roles of increasing faith and increasing commitment are shaped by sound and biblically based leadership.

One of the keys to sustaining this movement is to develop a culture of coaching that makes it normal for experienced leaders to equip emerging leaders to expand the vision and witness.

The Benefits of Coaching

Coaching is a blessing to any leader who will submit himself or herself to this personal discipline of growing from within. For years we heard about mentoring as an important discipline for self-growth. It is a powerful iron-sharpening-iron approach where a more-experienced leader pours into a less-experienced person by sharing experience and wisdom.

On the other hand, while mentors tend to be the experts, coaching seeks to bring out of the person being coached a self-awareness and a skill set that is resident in the person being coached. Coaching brings out the best in us because the coach is not telling us how, but is leading us to discover on our own our answers, strategy, and self-awareness.

There are many helpful resources available that teach coaching strategies. The International Coach Federation (ICF) is the gold standard for certification of coaches. Numerous books, podcasts, webinars, and workshops are available for different types and styles of coaching. One thing that is common to all the types of coaching disciplines is that coaching, when done well, has as its foundational discipline the ability to ask powerful questions.

If you are looking for a practical resource to help incorporate coaching into your daily life, I recommend *The Coaching Habit: Say Less, Ask More & Change the Way You Lead Forever* by Michael Bungay Stanier. This resource frames seven powerful questions that cover many of the roles and settings that you will encounter in coaching.

Many of us who have been trained in traditional models of ministry and have been nurtured and taught by mentors. Healthy models of ministry should not only include a mentor and coach but also a pastor, a therapist, a spiritual director, and a truth-telling friend. What do these people have to do with resurgence? Everything! Resurgence requires you to under-take courageous self-transformation for which we need advice, counsel, and reflection from outside trusted sources. The Bible encourages us by reminding us that there is wisdom in being surrounded by wise counsel.

I (Rodney) have the privilege of serving as coach to some of the most successful leaders in the church. Coaching is a two-way sword, and I say that with the best of intent. Watching these phenomenal leaders experience that "aha moment" in coaching and then execute that revelation in a way that takes their organization to the next level is an incredible experience. I don't know any successful leaders who don't have someone in the background assisting them to dream, cast vision, listen to new ideas, and encourage them to live fully into God's preferred future.

Coaching is also a safe space to think out loud and to get the type of feedback that clarifies processes and strategy. It is not counseling, therapy, or consultation. It is a learning and leadership discipline that allows you to listen to the Holy Spirit's direction and combines hindsight, insight, and foresight for a positive future outcome.

Many of my coaching clients' leadership skills have exponentially increased to the point that their churches and other organizations pay for coaching sessions as a proven benefit to the organizations' forward movement. Resurgence is driven by the effectiveness of the leaders of the organization. Consequently, group coaching, leadership team coaching, and systems and strategy coaching are common.

Resurgence leaders benefit from coaching because having the right coach can lead to resources, proven strategies, and best practices. Having the right coach also contributes to creating learning networks with other leaders who are seeking to move their organizations to the next level of learning and leadership.

I (Candace) have benefitted in my ministry journey by having excellent coaches, mentors, executive coaches, and resource people who have given me feedback at critical junctures in my life and ministry. I can say with confidence that without their feedback, coaching, and asking me the right question at the right time, I would not be where I am today.

God has used mentors and coaches to help mature me in ministry. Two in particular are the Reverend Geraldine McClellan, ordained elder in the Florida Annual Conference, and the Reverend Dr. Renita J. Weems, author, professor, and current vice president of the American Baptist College in Nashville, Tennessee.

Rev. McClellan was the first black clergywoman ordained by The United Methodist Church after being denied five times by the board of ordained ministry. Her sheer strength, tenacity, resilience, and tough words yet gentle spirit have guided me throughout my years in ministry.

Rev. McClellan was the first female clergy I spoke to when I sensed God calling me to full-time ministry. She is close to retirement now, but we still talk almost weekly. I can call her whenever I'm challenged, and she continues to share her wisdom. She is a shoulder to cry on whenever needed.

Rev. Dr. Weems has mentored and coached me from a distance through the books she's written. Four of my favorites are *Just a Sister Away, I Asked for Intimacy, Listening for*

God: A Minister's Journey Through Silence and Doubt, and What Matters Most.

While living in Nashville, I attended Ray of Hope Community Church regularly, which Rev. Dr. Weems co-pastors with Rev. Martin Espinosa. She mentored me through her preaching and prayed for me often on the altar as I cried out to God. She coached me through my application process when I submitted for the executive director's positon in our denomination's New Church Start Division.

I was the first woman and person of color hired to lead our denomination's church planting movement. Rev. Dr. Weems corrected me when I said, "They gave me the job." She told me that power concedes nothing. Instead, "you earned the job, Candace."

Rev. Dr. Weems's feedback has always been invaluable. She once said, "As a woman in leadership, you don't get what you deserve. You get what you negotiate." She explained that as a clergywoman the importance of not putting all your eggs in one basket by saying, "It's a mighty poor mouse that only has one hole for the cheese."

Rev. Dr. Weems spoke at an event we hosted called "Lead Like a Woman and Not Like a Girl." She shared the realities that women in ministry face dealing with sexism, inequities, and power dynamics. She reassured us that we could navigate these realities if we acknowledge their existence and not put our proverbial heads in the sand. She affirmed that we are women called by God to lead and to serve.

I am grateful for the many coaches and mentors God sent into my life. And I am especially grateful for Rev. McClellan and Rev. Dr. Weems. To the clergywomen who are reading this resource, don't try to go it alone! Connect with quality clergy sisters who will support you along this journey called life and ministry.

Conclusion

There are several foundational keys to becoming a coaching leader:

- Coaching leaders need a coach themselves.
- Coaching is best learned by experience.
- Effective coaching leaders create or join networks of leaders who share resources and best practices.
- Coaching leaders become lifelong learners.

Reflect and Respond

1. What do you view as your primary role in relationship to the people in the church?

2. Is your job to tell everyone what to do or to empower others to see what needs to be done and then get it done?

3. The greatest act of stewardship that we can give is the gift of identifying and training new leaders for spiritual and community service. We should plan to invest with intentionality in providing training and facilitation for leadership development.

4. Coaching creates new community. What are the things that you should seek to learn from coaching based on learning environments?

5. Learning to network is a benefit of coaching. What are the benefits of building a network related to your ministry roles and responsibilities?

6. Coaching creates a life-long learning environment. Why and how is life-long learning important in resurgent ministries?

Action Items: Our investment of time, talent, gifts, service, and witness toward present and future leaders is a long-term viability. Resurgence requires investments today for returns tomorrow. Scholarships, internships, fellowships, and other intentional sources of creating a culture of leadership development should be one of the foundational principles for resurgence.

Partnerships with other learning communities; community colleges, online learning centers, advocacy-learning organizations, neighborhood schools, cooperate training centers, and denominational learning assets are vital to growing our influence as a community asset.

Coaching creates an environment for self-awareness and continuous self-improvement. The traits for leadership are helpful because they set in motion communities of creative and innovative service.

Another benefit of coaching is the continuous flow of new resources that are shared. These resources enhance a leader's ability to mature and develop others for more effective service. Coaching also creates accountability and care. It assists leaders in setting and achieving goals and demonstrates healthy collegiality. Coaching is not just about clergy; it is about building healthy teams at all levels of our organizations.

Throughout the seasons of church growth and vitality, plans and programs have come and gone. I believe that coaching will be around for a long time because it helps us as leaders to improve. It gives us the tools to empower our congregations for long-term vitality and seeds a skill set for future generations to benefit from the investment of those who have preceded them.

Several years ago, I read the forward in Pat Robertson's book, *Shout It From The Housetop*, that said, "Attempt something so big, that unless God intervenes it's bound to fail." Coaching helps us find the courage to ask the tough questions and teaches us how to patiently wait until God's answer is revealed through that legion of angels God sends to us, even though we are sometimes unaware.

CHAPTER 7

From Scarcity to Abundance: Funding Resurgence

Elisha replied to her, "How can I help you? Tell me, what do you have in your house? Your servant has nothing there at all," she said, "except a small jar of olive oil." – 2 Kings 4:2 (NIV)

The biblical story of the widow and God's divine provisions found in 2 Kings 4 is one that I've seen fulfilled personally. My (Candace's) mother became a widow in 2003 when my father died unexpectedly of a massive heart attack. Even though all her children were adults and living on their own at the time, my mom still had debt she and my dad had incurred.

Mom has always been a woman of prayer and faith and believed God would provide. She tells us the story of reading the Scripture from 2 Kings 4 and in faith asking God as a widow to show her the "oil" of provisions she had that God could miraculously multiply. She said she put out a "jar" in faith and prayed for months for provision to pay her debts.

One day after prayer, Mom was sitting on her porch looking at the vacant rental property in need of repair that she now owned since Dad's death. As she sat looking at the property, a man drove up, got out of his car, and started inspecting the property. He asked for the name of the owner. Mom responded that she was the owner.

The man explained that he was interested in purchasing the property as is. Within a few months, my mother signed the closing paperwork, and the property sold for the amount of money needed to pay her debts, with additional funds left to cover living expenses. She testifies that often we don't see the oil that God has given us that only God can miraculously multiply.

Once we've identified our oil, that small provision that we have that God can miraculously multiply, we then have to collect and set out jars in faith. If the widow had placed before God only a few jars, only a few would have been filled.

Mom was honest about the needs she had and asked God for provision to be debt-free. God showed her the oil she had in the unrepaired property. The miracle was sending a buyer who would purchase it as is, without her having to find the money to bring it up to city code before she could list the property for sale. The sale price was more than fair, which further confirmed for Mom that it was God's miraculous provision.

God wants to move us from a place and mindset of scarcity to abundance. We have to join God in faith and remember that everything belongs to God. God asks us to be faithful stewards over God's possessions.

> Yours, O LORD, are the greatness, the power, the
> glory, the victory, and the majesty; for all that is
> in the heavens and on the earth is yours; yours
> is the kingdom, O LORD, and you are exalted as
> head above all. Riches and honor come from you,
> and you rule over all. In your hand are power and
> might; and it is in your hand to make great and
> to give strength to all. And now, our God, we give
> thanks to you and praise your glorious name.
> – 2 Chronicles 29:11-13

This chapter brings to light the subject of stewardship and how we as church pastors and leaders can move from a mindset of scarcity to abundance, believing that God can fund the church's resurgence. As we thought about "Who could do this with us?" we consulted with Cedric D. Lewis, a faithful United Methodist lay person who has earned an MBA and a MACC. He is also an accounting professional and instructor with over 25 years of experience in the corporate, private for-profit, and not-for-profit sectors. We enjoyed collaborating with him on this chapter and are honored to include his input.

As we talk about moving from scarcity to abundance, we know we have to lead with humility, respect, and faith with this subject. We recognize that people come from different places and life experiences. Some have experienced real poverty, so a scarcity mindset is not one to be mocked but respected.

We must understand that an abundance mindset is not for self-consumption of a prosperity mindset but to abundantly share with others. When we understand that everything belongs to God and we are offered opportunities to be stewards of God's creation, we can embrace an abundance mindset and bless others, thereby reflecting God's generosity.

Scarcity	Abundance
dependent on self	willingness to depend on God and to ask for and receive help from the people of God
limit to what a person can see, create, manufacture, give, or do to his or her own ideas	awareness of God's ownership of everything; and one's ability to see, manufacture, give, or do can be multiplied when aligned with others who are willing to help

Scarcity	Abundance
rooted in fears based on real-life experiences of lack and not enough provisions; also a fear of failure or rejection, which often prevents a person from asking for help	rooted in understanding the unlimited nature of God and God's expectation that we be good stewards of God's creation and gifts (knowledge that there is more where that came from) and a willingness to take risks with the guidance of those who are serving communities
experienced in the life-cycle of poverty; little to no experience or exposure to authentically generous people	not selfish (recognition that everyone is a resource for accomplishing God's will) and being willing to go outside of any existing comfort zone to become a vital congregation
impacted greatly by unjust systems in our society and often feels powerless	acknowledges the unjust systems in society and has joined forces with others to work toward collective change for self and the community
mindset that controls and rations everything	generosity as a lifestyle

Moving from scarcity to abundance requires:

- A change in mindset that acknowledges God has the resources needed and God gives those resources through God's people.
- Understanding that our paths forward and solutions can be limited by our own experiences and that others can help and are willing to help. We need to acknowledge the limits of our own ideas and be

willing to consider others' ideas inside and outside of the congregation.

- Being willing to take risks based on the counsel of others. New things require new risks, especially those that are supported by others in and outside of the congregation.
- Understanding that the path to becoming a resurging vital congregation will be uncomfortable and sometimes painful. Abundance requires us to allow others to share in bearing our burdens, holding our hands, guiding us, and encouraging us as we exit our comfort zones.
- Accepting that many outside of our congregations and communities served and still serve alongside us to confront, change, and thrive in spite of unjust systems.
- Being willing to live a generous lifestyle where giving to those inside and outside of the congregation and community will ultimately help build the kingdom of God.

Generosity and Stewardship: Two Sides of the Same Coin

Generosity involves the giver (our worship and obedience to God and willingness to give to our brothers and sisters). Stewardship involves the receiver (our worship to God and accountability to God and our brothers and sisters) and how we put to use what has been entrusted to us.

Generosity is the term that I prefer to use, but *stewardship* is also at the heart of this discussion. Scripture reminds us that where our treasure is, that's also where our heart is. Any type of change from the status quo to something new is going to involve and invent new resources. Time, talents, gifts, service, and witness are all components of stewardship. The challenge now is to invite people in the pews to invest in their future. Motivational sermons and great communication, as well as practical and insightful invitations for involvement, all create healthy platforms for increased generosity in the life of the church.

Generosity is a lifestyle and spiritual discipline that is directly connected to thankfulness for what God has done in our lives. The gratitude we express undergirds our response of demonstrated appreciation for what God has already done on our behalf.

Generosity must be taught and nurtured for it to become a forward movement in the life of the church. Generosity is taught and shaped through sermons, church school, pulpit mission moments, and a host of other learning opportunities and resources; and it involves freely giving our time, talents, gifts, service, and witness. These five "jars" of involvement in ministry are the framework through which people find their way into faithful service and witness.

When we learn the gift of generosity, then we can invest beyond the walls of the local church. Generosity is also a spiritual gift for some; and regardless of whether some saints have it, all people still give where their hearts lead them.

Resurgence ministry involves a high degree of commitment. It can only happen in places where there is a culture of high commitment and an expectation of involvement at every level, within and beyond the walls of the church.

Understanding Generosity

Generosity is simply understanding God as the source of our provisions. When we give, we are returning to God a portion of what God has already given to us. We are simply stewards—caretakers of God's resources. When we begin to understand the joy of being asked to be a steward, it manifests in the privilege of returning back to God what God has entrusted to our care.

The word *generosity* reflects a positive outlook for our giving and a positive response to God's generosity toward us, and it requires spiritual maturity. Churches that practice generosity are taught with regularity the relationship between thanksgiving, commitment, and blessings as a result of our discipled commitment to abundant giving.

Generosity is also a spiritual gift in the body of Christ. Romans 12:6-8 says, "We have different gifts, according to the grace given to each of us. If your gift is prophesying, then prophesy in accordance with your faith; if it is serving, then serve; if it is teaching, then teach; if it is to encourage, then give encouragement; if it is giving, then give generously."

Congregations seeking to experience resurgence may have members who have the spiritual gift of giving and may or may not know it. But for those members who do have this gift, a resurgence-focused congregations would not have to ask them to ask for contributions above their sustained tithes because they can be relied upon to give as they have been in the past.

However, some members with the spiritual gift of giving may have had their spirits quenched because in the past they felt taken advantage of or taken for granted. As with all spiritual gifts, the Spirit must flow. Resurgent congregations should take care to ensure that those with this spiritual gift are nurtured through Bible studies like Kenneth Cain Kinghorn's *Gifts of the Spirit* and free spiritual gifts inventory sites like *spiritualgiftstest.com/#1485358831660-9f25e9b5-029c*.

Teaching and preaching on personal stewardship and generosity (the discipline of personal budgeting, tithing as a sustained giving practice, first-fruit giving as an increase over the tithe, and sacrificial giving as a top-tier priority) are all vital for a resurgent congregation. What these strategies have in common is sustained examples through teaching, preaching, generosity testimonies, and celebration of giving. Teaching and preaching about generous giving should become an organic part of all resurgent churches to the point that the members are teaching and encouraging one another in the spiritual discipline. Members who are excited about and understand generous giving can then teach and disciple new members.

If you as a leader don't personally feel comfortable in teaching and preaching about generosity and stewardship, consider inviting someone who is to resource your ministry on an ongoing basis. A minimum of once per quarter, there should be an intentional focus on generosity and stewardship in your ministry. Little or no resurgence can occur in the church until the ministry of generous giving is brought front and center.

One of the signs of decline in a church is diminishing financial resources. Pastor and laity often recognize these stages of decline but often feel helpless and subsequently accept the results of decline without mounting an aggressive strategy to reverse it.

Clergy often feel uncomfortable preaching and teaching about stewardship. There are three reasons for this. First, we feel inadequate in our knowledge of the subject and do not always model good stewardship practices for the congregation in our own lives. Second, we incorrectly believe that the people in the pews will be offended if we preach on stewardship. Third, we personally are not practicing total lifestyle stewardship.

In my opinion, stewardship is one of the hardest disciplines to learn as a spiritual leader. In my early ministry, I was not living fully in faithful personal giving and was afraid that preaching about money would not be received well by the congregation. I just didn't have a good grasp of the concepts of generosity and stewardship.

As I moved to larger ministry responsibilities, I reached out to more mature pastoral and lay leaders who said the same things. Look at God's plan for provision: sowing and reaping, faith and obedience, and discipline and sacrifice. When I started practicing these things, teaching the principles and preaching the whole gospel of the Bible's wise counsel in these areas, I began to see the people mature and the giving increase. I recommend that leaders who want their ministries to improve in this area, invest in a biblically based stewardship seminar to learn stewardship Scriptures, become familiar with proven strategies, and increase their personal commitment to abundant giving.

Crown Ministries financial Bible studies and Dave Ramsey's Financial Peace programs are excellent examples of Bible-based comprehensive and effective personal money management studies available to clergy and laity. These programs allow laity to teach others how to better manage personal finances and, thereby, make room for what they will contribute to the ministry of their congregation. When clergy and members become better stewards of the resources God has entrusted to them, they can be better stewards of the collective resources God gives to congregations.

Generous giving should never be seen as a burden, but it should be seen as a blessing. Our language and our witness about giving should always reflect the joy of generosity and therefore reflect an ongoing invitation to support the ministries of the church with our financial resources.

"Where there is no vision the people perish" (Proverbs 29:18). When there are no clear and vital ministry programs, the people will not give to the church; and when members hear sermons about stewardship, they very well may wonder why they are feeling guilty about not giving to a congregation that they cannot clearly see where the funds are going, other than operations. While it is true that where my treasure is there my heart is, it is also true that my treasure is where it is because someone or some cause gave my heart a reason to put it there.

As a layperson with over 16 years of experience in serving local churches in the area of finance, serving on not-for-profit boards as treasurer, as well as serving in the not-for-profit sector as a financial professional, I (Cedric) believe churches can benefit from some of the best practices of the larger secular not-for-profit (NFP) sector of which they are a part. All thriving and financially resourceful NFPs must articulate their vision, mission, and programs clearly to the public in order to receive financial support.

NFPs use a combination of storytelling and accountability reporting to enlist the support of donors. Resurgence focused churches must do the same by enlisting clergy and laity in prayerfully identifying community and congregational needs and prioritizing which of those needs it will seek to meet. Resurgent congregations can then clearly and authentically communicate the financial needs of the church on a regular basis without guilt, shame, or disappointment. People will give to meet needs.

Generous giving involves more than money. It is a spiritual discipline that involves our time, talents, gifts, service, and witness. Over the years, I (Rodney) have moved away from using the term *stewardship* when I am speaking in the context of giving. I've replaced it with the term *generosity*.

One of my favorite pastoral sermons on stewardship is based on Matthew 14:13-21, generally known as "The Feeding of the Five Thousand." I have always titled that sermon "The Generosity Factor." My teaching points from that sermon are: The Miracle of Compassion, The Miracle of Community, and The Miracle of Communion.

The point of the sermon is that God provides all kinds of settings to experience generosity in our midst. When we care for God's people, we find ways to be a resource to them. When we create shared community, we always have more than enough. And when we gather in worship and celebrate God's provision, our generosity manifests in everyone being blessed.

While I don't encourage preaching other pastors' sermons, today there are several online resources available to assist you in your preparation for preaching great sermons on generosity and stewardship.

Fundraising and Generous Giving: A Necessity for Resurging Churches

As is true in the NFP sector, the primary funding source outside of government and private grants is fundraising. All churches should do it whether they need to or not because effective fundraising involves a specific campaign with a specific fund goal within a specific span of time and can use multiple options within the campaign.

Churches have successfully used these principles for much of the 21st century. For example, a building campaign may seek to raise funds to help retrofit the Sunday school area to be more flexible space so a resurgent church can support the needs of its community (12-step programs, community groups, sororities, fraternities, civic groups, for example) The campaign may have a goal of $75,000 and a one-year target date. The resurgent church may plan to have dinner sales, car washes, candy sales, member pledges, and benefactor gifts to help raise those funds.

Fundraising has spiritual and practical benefits. Spiritually, for a specific period of time, the congregation is singularly focused on this one goal. As such, members can be invited to pray during the campaign, promote Bible study, and experience unity of mind and spirit. We saw this at New Life when the church decided to move its worship facility from a built-out storefront shopping center to a traditional church building and campus. A practical benefit of such fundraising is that all members are working on a single goal, which increases the faith and the probability of everyone that the goal will be achieved.

Resurgent churches can also model fundraising in the NFP sector by focusing it on one or two well publicized and well executed events that invite the community to participate. Of three well known NFPs that I have worked closely with, one raised 30 percent of its annual operating budget in one event; a second raised 50 percent of its operating budget in one event; and a third raised 80 percent of its operating budget in two fundraising galas.

I (Rodney) have never been a chicken, fish, and barbecue fundraising advocate. I have always thought that the effort given to cook and sell the food could be replaced with people just giving the money that was spent on the food and distribution of the dinners. This does not have to be the case.

Fundraising for a resurgent church and abundant thinking allow for many fundraising events to help meet the goal, so there is no single path. Furthermore, many enjoy the culturally rich (and sometimes salty) flavor of "church food." A well-planned food event can range from preparing and selling chicken, fish, and barbecue every Saturday afternoon for the next year to having a dinner or gala at the church or a community center, whereby the church and the community are engaged with each other.

At New Life, we (Candace and congregation) did so much chicken, fish, and barbeque that the Saturday meal became known as "The Grille" in the church and the community. This fundraising event also allowed many in the church and the community to fellowship, pray, and support one another.

The Grille became so popular that we took orders from patrons in nearby hair salons and barbershops, and we delivered. We even created menus with a variety of choices that included tender ribs and creamy coleslaw. Using terms like these helped to set the customer's expectations of what they were getting and helped sell more dinners.

Profits of church meals can range anywhere from 20 to 90 percent. The higher profitable events tend to have more of the food items donated by members, who receive an in-kind charitable donation letter from the church, thereby, allowing the church to receive all dinner receipts as profit. Some believe that the effort involved in church food fundraising outweighs the financial benefit. However, any NFP would be grateful to receive similar fundraising receipts weekly, especially from a group of volunteers.

In Matthew 14:13-21, Jesus and the disciples fed at least 5,000 people. The resurgent church of the 21st century that sells an average of 100 meals (fried fish, french fries, and coleslaw) for 52 weeks can meet the needs of the community and earn funds to support ministry in the process.

Resurgent churches that are willing to experience God's abundance will not limit their fundraising efforts to known tried-and-true fundraisers alone. They will unapologetically use their known resources as part of the path to achieving the goal. Therefore, fundraising can be a means to get resurgent church members reengaged in giving to their church.

Many resurgent churches have an abundance of unused space that could be put to use by the community. Resurgent churches that have unused education space can connect with the arts, an unused fellowship hall could become a dance studio, or a church with a stage could become a community playhouse.

Many communities have needs to just have meeting space within the neighborhood. Twelve-step programs (Alcoholics Anonymous, Gamblers Anonymous, Narcotics Anonymous, for example) are organic, self-organizing, and self-sustaining groups that simply need a safe place to meet, and they may be willing to make a small donation to the church.

Members of the congregation who are interested in volunteering their time and talents might wish to set up coffee and cookies an hour before the meetings begin. This kind of experience reconnects resurgent church members with generous giving in all forms.

The resurgent church can put up signs outside of their church, advertising free or reduced rent for space. They can post ads on Craigslist, and many community newspapers will give churches discounts or will not charge for this kind of advertising.

Regular biblical teaching in small-group ministry, leadership training, and leadership settings, along with enthusiastic emphasis from the pulpit must undergird and come before the appeal for financial support of our ministries. Ministry leaders should inspire people to be engaged in impactful community and discipleship ministry. People need vision and the freedom to envision impactful ministry and ministry needs.

Most of ministry is storytelling. It's the telling of our past victories and our present opportunities that shape the possibilities for our future. We are storytelling people. Placing stories before us provides pictures of what can fuel our faith. If we are not vision-focused, then our people won't be vision-focused. Our role as spiritually mature leaders is to help people see the future.

Before one shovel of dirt was turned for the construction of the new ministry center at Central Church, I (Rodney), invited people during a sermon when they headed toward the parking lot to see the new building. In fact, I asked them to see that someone had left the light on in the restroom on the top floor of the new building. I watched as they turned the corner of the sanctuary and they saw the new building in that spot for themselves. Once people can see where their treasure is going and how beneficial their treasure is to a project, their hearts will respond in kind.

The invitation to generosity should come frequently and must be a priority for a resurgent church. This requires the ministry leaders to be aligned with the priorities of their communities.

If the resurgent church wants to help improve the safety of its neighborhood, then the church can become the meeting place for the neighborhood watch/walkers. The church could help lead the efforts in raising money for flashlights, walkie-talkies, and reflective vests they use. When impactful community and discipleship ministry is happening in a church, then the reason to raise money for church operations becomes clear.

Churches could also provide space for annual back-to-school community events; carnivals; summer camps; block parties; cookouts; and sporting events. Remember, the heart responds with treasure when the heart sees a clear path to where the treasure is going. A generous church is a blessed church. Even resurgent churches should give to other churches its time, talent, and resources, so find ways to give to other resurgent churches.

As United Methodists, we form partnerships with ministry and mission through our connectional giving. This generosity of sharing with other congregations throughout the denomination enables us to have a global impact on ministry and mission. As this resource goes to press, our connectional giving is supporting natural disaster relief domestically and abroad. As the expression goes, "Many hands make light work."

Ministries that are healthy financially consistently invite their members to act in faith in their giving and vision for God's preferred future for their ministry and community. Generosity is our response to God's faithful care of us.

Throughout this resource we have asked, "Who will do this with us?" The day of congregations operating as silos is behind us. We should be in partnerships with our brothers and sisters in ministry within and beyond our connectional partners. Generous giving extends past resurgent congregations and connects to surging congregations.

Beyond our focus on Sunday morning worship, we must see ourselves as resource centers in more ways than just worship service on Sunday. One of our greatest assets is our facilities, which can be shared as resource generators between the Sundays. They can be used as schools, training centers, meeting facilities, athletic and banquet centers, shared worship space, office and meeting areas, support groups, scouts, and community organizations. The list of potential revenue and missional use is endless.

Last but not least, we must educate our members about how they can give generously past their earthly years through will designations, estate endowments, and bequeaths. There are many resources available through our denominational agencies that can assist us with this training.

The Importance of Stewardship

Stewardship involves our worshiping God through intentional and transparent accountability to God and our

127

brothers and sisters for what has been given to us. A resurgent congregation that has actively engaged in teaching generous giving, that has inspired members to do community and discipleship impactful ministries, must make plans to execute the plans. There must be two planning paths: one for impactful ministry and one for sustained operations.

An annual conference and a district can support the operational path by generously giving to keep the operations of the resurgent church open for several years with accountability. A best practice in the NFP sector for grants that provide operational support is matching grants. This is where a donor matches the amount a NFP can raise on its own.

Resurgent churches should be supported in scaling back operating expenses to a level that the congregation could sustain if their current giving level was matched by the conference or the district. For example, if a resurgent congregation is giving $5,000 monthly toward operations, a conference or a district may wish to match that amount. This helps ensure that the conference or the district is not giving beyond what the resurgent congregation is willing to engage in. As the congregation's giving increases, the conference or the district's match should also increase by the same amount. This can serve as a motivator for the resurgent congregation.

If the resurgent congregation's giving decreases, the matched amount should also decrease. This helps the resurgent congregation think clearly about its spending priorities.

Once a matching agreement has been met, the resurgent congregation will need to prepare an operating budget as well as a community and discipleship impact budget. It's important to prepare a realistic budget that has input from a wide range of people in the ministry, including the wisdom and expertise of generous givers from a resurging church. Education to the larger congregation regarding the purpose and strategic focus of budget priorities must be done in writing and connected to the vision and purpose of the ministry.

A resurging congregation must be guided in prayerful, supportive, and meaningful planning sessions where all voices are allowed to be heard. This can be a difficult time for some in the resurgent congregation, so those who are supporting must give care. The planning meetings must be designed to allow the resurging congregation to be empowered and all of their voices to be heard. Central questions that must be answered are, "Given our community and discipleship impact events, what amount of resources will be needed to sustain the congregation until those events can be executed? And how many resources will be needed to actually execute those events?"

With two planning paths of operations and impactful ministry, many churches use the fall months of the year to create the two path budgets that begin in January. Vital congregations monitor the cycles of giving in their churches and know the most fruitful and lean seasons of giving. The first category, buy-in and ownership of the budget priorities, should be reflected by several areas of emphasis: fixed costs, utilities, salaries and benefits, conference, district, general church, missional, and community partnership support. The second category of emphasis should focus on the long-term support (savings and investments), and the third should reflect emerging ministry opportunities.

As it relates to emerging ministry opportunities, new ministries are those that will develop in stages or phases. Some of that funding is reflected in the present budget; some of it is reflected in the future budget. Some of the resources come from the pews, while other resources come from our ministry partners.

Even with operational budgets, there are four things that will ensure an increase in giving in the life of your congregation: (1) Connect the giving to God's vision for your ministry. People will give to a sustained realistic appeal that shows growth in the ministry. (2) Make certain that your reporting of the giving is accurate and sustained. Make monthly reports to the congregation of the planning and giving activities and how everyone can be a part. Provide members with quarterly giving statements, informing the members of the progress of their giving and provide them with checkpoints to catch up and increase their giving. (3) Share testimonies of blessings of the faithfulness of giving, and encourage others to share their blessings with others. (4) Be exceptionally missional and generous with appropriate giving opportunities beyond the doors of your church.

With regard to the operational path, members can be invited to pledge to cover certain expenses as one-time gifts or over the course of a few months. Nevertheless, the two-path budgeting process (operations and impactful ministry) must be accompanied with substantial accountability.

Funds that are designated for ministry must not be used for operations without serious counsel and wisdom from the ministry stakeholders. If people are giving to ministry and the lights are at risk of being turned off, then the congregation must know as far in advance as is possible. Decisions to use ministry funds during times of resurgence should not be left to the church council or the finance committee. Trust of the people leading the stewardship process and trust in the stewardship reporting process is vital during this time.

It can also be helpful for a resurgent congregation to use computerized accounting software like QuickBooks. A partnership with a resurging congregation could be reached to provide a computer, software, and training. As the congregation becomes more self-sustaining, its reliance on a partner congregation will diminish; however, the blessings of generous giving will remain.

The lifeblood of our future is the biblical concept that we are stewards, not owners of the things of God. The generosity factor has to become a common thread in our investment for the long-term fruit bearing for the church. We have been entrusted to be faithful stewards of things we don't own but are blessed to receive them.

Generosity In The Digital Age

Resurgence ministries understand that giving in support of local ministries and global mission involves several strategies. Healthy ministries are incorporating several methods of giving into the worship and mission experience. In addition to the traditional passing of the plate and mail in giving, new forms of giving include, on-line giving, direct deposit, church giving apps, and portable giving kiosks.

Following trends in modern society, the more options that are presented to givers, the greater the potential for them to support ministries generously. Some people simply don't carry a lot of cash on them anymore. There are people who don't use checks and handle most of their financial transactions with credit and debit cards. Churches that provide these options for giving are reporting significant increases in receipts of tithes and offerings.

Electronic and physical giving will increase only if accompanied by robust educational, missional and spiritual teaching on giving. As a pastor I (Rodney) have employed many strategies to increase giving. We cannot be timid about preaching and teaching on biblical stewardship. One method that I have found to be exceptionally effective is to use a multi-level approach. Preach on generosity at least once per quarter, tell stories of the positive impact on generous every chance you get by sharing testimonies through your communications portals. Celebration of generosity always increases giving.

Generosity is directly tied to spiritual maturity and missions. When people grow in their knowledge as disciples of Christ they also grow in their responsibilities to support ministries with their time, talents, gifts, service and witness. When people can see the benefits of their generosity, increased giving will occur.

With a growing trend in on-line viewing, new skills are needed to make appeals to the viewing worshippers just as if they are sitting in the pews — and they are. Invitational language that makes the viewers sense that they are not just remote but worshipping from differently locations causes them to give generosity also.

Resurgence also invites giving from our ministry partners and supporters who though they may not be members of the church, are moved by the Holy Spirit to support the work and impact of the ministry. Everyday people are asked to support organizations, causes and events. They respond generously because they have been asked. As we navigate the future of giving in the local church, our reality is that every dime and dollar we receive will not just come from the local offering plate. Our strategy for resurgence must involve additional streams of financial support being receiving both from traditional and non-traditional means. Prayerfully consider how to expand your giving appeal.

Conclusion

Generosity is about more than just survival. Generosity is living into the promises of God through growing faithful and mature givers who see themselves as God's instruments, blessed to give to support ministry.

A primary tool of resurgence is increased church giving. Being good stewards of God's financial resources is a discipline that begins when pastoral leadership is fulfilled with a mature lay leadership culture and lived out with faithful stewardship.

In our own way, this imperfect resource is a way for us to give back some of our experience, commitment, and shared wisdom so that others can benefit from the gifts and labor of others who have preceded us on the journey. Resurgent ministries have at their heart a desire to survive so that they can be a launch pad for something that is yet to come.

When others raise the question, "Is the church dying?" resurgent ministries change the narrative from death to resurrection. It's not about us. It's for the generations who will follow us. We make the sacrifice today to ensure that the church will be around tomorrow.

Stewardship is a response to God and to His people.

At the heart of Resurgence ministries is sound biblical teaching on tithing and first-fruits giving. While the tithe represents a tenth, First Fruits means to set aside the very best of our resources as an offering to God, this gift often exceeds the tithe.

In addition to passing the plate, and mail in giving options, modern forms of giving include on-line giving, direct deposit, church giving apps, portable kiosks and memorial giving options. These new giving options will result in increased giving when they are accompanied by preaching and teaching on biblical stewardship. Resurgence leaders frequently connect stories of generosity with opportunities to motivate others to increase giving.

With an increase in digital viewing options, we have to increase our appeal for both discipleship and financial resources with invitational language that is not just for the people who are present in the sanctuary, but also for those viewing on-line. This giving appeal is cultivated and communicated through sound biblical principles that invite worshippers to incorporate generous giving into their spiritual disciplines along with prayer, bible reading, missions, worship, service, and witness.

CHAPTER 8

From Membership to Discipleship

Then Jesus came to them and said, "All authority in heaven and on earth has been given to me. Therefore go and make disciples of all nations, baptizing them in the name of the Father and of the Son and of the Holy Spirit, and teaching them to obey everything I have commanded you. And surely I am with you always, to the very end of the age." – Matthew 28:18-20 (NIV)

There are a number of great resources that focus on growing church membership, and there are great resources that focus on creating a discipleship culture. Only recently has there been a major focus on connecting these two themes into a single discussion. We believe three things are driving this emerging discussion.

First, a growing number of churches are facing the reality that membership is not as important to worship participants as it once was and that there has been a societal change that is lessening the necessity of joining organizations that undermines the membership model. Second, a growing diversity around church backgrounds is creating an environment where it's no longer uncommon for individuals and families to actively participate in more than one congregation on an ongoing basis.

Third, some churches are better at delivering some types of ministries and missions than others. This is especially true around children and youth activities. The result: Membership is only as important as the access it provides to the participants.

Megachurches are now maturing to the point where they are seeing that one size doesn't fit all. They are also like all size churches attempting to recapture the importance of small groups within the large worship attendance models. Once the music stops and the preaching ceases, people are still attracted to churches by intimate community. This is a foundational principle for new church starts as well as for established ministries. It is even harder in established ministries because friendships and long-term relationships make it more difficult to include new people.

At the heart of all growing and vital ministries is an intentional focus on creating the intimate feel of small groups within the larger gathering of worship. The biblical model for this is found in Acts 2:42-46 (CEB):

> The believers devoted themselves to the apostles' teaching, to their shared meals, and to their prayers. A sense of awe came over everyone. God performed many wonders and signs through the apostles. All the believers were united and shared everything. They would sell pieces of property and possessions and distribute the proceeds to everyone who needed them. Every day, they met together in the temple and ate in their homes. They shared food with gladness and simplicity. They praised God and demonstrated God's goodness to everyone. The Lord added daily to the community those who were being saved.

Resurgence invites a fresh look at how we do ministry with people who are transient by design. The membership model no longer guarantees commitment nor loyalty to a single congregation. Add to this equation competition from Sunday athletic, social, and family events, and it changes the landscape of traditional membership requirements.

Sunday school may need to be replaced by mid-week online educational communities. Board meetings my need to take place over social media. Worship services may need to be broadcast on the web. In the past, membership ensured a place to be baptized, married, and buried. In today's society, the thought of being a lifelong member of a single congregation is not as common.

While discipleship models are not new to the church, they are absolutely essential to maturing disciples for the work of ministry. It's impossible to take a church to the next level without a curriculum that intentionally defines what that maturity of spiritual growth looks like. Even our GPS devices have at the heart of their operating systems consistent coordinates that define the latitude and longitude of their position. A discipleship plan is key to resurgence because "without a vision the people perish."

Resurgence does not ignore the tried and true. Instead, it creates an awareness that we must become self-aware of changing trends. Those changing trends create new opportunities to move the core values of traditional church models into relevant delivery systems for today and tomorrow. Disciple-based systems create strategies to assist persons in discovering their current location and to evolve to new places in their journey.

Resurgence is a great platform to pivot to discipleship models where people are developed for Kingdom growth and not just congregational growth. Resurgence invites us to take proven strategies and translate some of them into innovative ways to build new approaches to effective ministry.

An example of this is use of web-based platforms to host online Bible study, administrative meetings, and collaborative meetings, and teachings. A resurgence model would ask, "What would happen if a ministry across town is doing a discipleship training that can be shared with several churches through social media collaboration?" One of the foundational messages of resurgence is "Who will do this with me?" As Methodists, we can bring back an undated model of the early Methodist class systems: societies and bands with technological bridges that allow us to share resources on-demand.

Discipleship systems can be shared through podcasting, webinars, and teaching on-demand. Pastors and teachers can share their skills beyond the doors of one local congregation and begin to think normatively about ministry clusters and learning communities. These models also address the elephant in the room: How will we afford to do this in our local church? The cost and ease of technology today is as affordable as a cell phone, tablet, or laptop computer.

An additional benefit of this approach is that it recreates the concept of parish ministry. United Methodists have one of the best connectional systems of ministry already in existence. Repurposing these systems with an intentional mindset of sharing discipleship resources will have as a natural outcome the building of connected faith communities. The resurgence models are already being used in communities through shared food co-ops, joint funding of community programs, and shared resourcing for larger community needs.

A New Way of Thinking

Growing churches understand discipleship is the churchs primary role, not just membership. In a time where membership and average worship attendance is declining, focus on discipleship and building systems that make discipleship happen is a strategic focus that is at the heart of resurgence.

Focus on membership alone will not connect churches with their expanding missional field. When you think about areas of potential growth in and around your ministry, where do you see new people coming from? Because of changing attendance patterns, we have to invest in new strategies to involve new people in ministry.

Resurgence explores current and future opportunities to connect with people and extend invitations to them to become involved with the church. Unlike the past when we often waited until people showed up at the church doors, today we have to take the church where the people are. Our "ministry of presence" reach in the community is often the on-ramp for many to future involvement with the church.

Many of our own ministries of invitation should be designated to attract people who are not already involved in ministry. In the past, we relied on evangelism taking place in our buildings, but today our evangelism efforts must include going where the people are.

Preparation and training for this type of outreach begins at the church but is accomplished in the community. Our emphasis on discipleship shifts our strategies to equip our members to go and invite others into relationship with Jesus Christ.

Internally, our offerings of programs, ministries, and services are the invitation points. Externally, our relationship building capacity is the invitation point. The Acts 2:42-46 model of discipleship-making enlarges the capacity to learn, teach, equip, and share as Christian community. Resurgence changes the narrative from that church or this church.

Impact United Methodist Church calls its campuses Impact on Sylvan Road and Impact on Main Street, both located in East Point, Georgia. They also model the benefit of reclaiming underused or abandoned properties that can be repurposed to expand ministry footprints.

Old First Church can grow again by offering ministry targeted to another generation of potential believers. Think of the possibilities if vital and growth congregations were given opportunities to develop additional places of ministry in communities that are experiencing cultural and social change.

St. Mark United Methodist Church in Wichita, Kansas, and its partner campus, Saint Mark Southeast Campus, are an example of how cross-cultural ministry can succeed. Windsor Village United Methodist Church and The Kingdom Builders' Center in Houston, Texas, are another example of a discipleship model that has a distinctive community, economic, social, and educational development component.

An effective discipleship system is one that is appropriate for membership and discipleship use.

Foundational to a Disciple-Making System

On mission to make disciples. It's impossible to experience resurgence with a membership-only model of ministry. The foundational teaching of resurgence is building Christ's kingdom through renewal and intentional making of new disciples for the transformation of the world.

Our focus for ministry in resurgence shifts our emphasis from solely taking care of those who are already members to ramping up our strategic focus to attract new people to the ministry. In other words, we should be intentional in dedicating ministry resources to nurturing and recruitment. Resurgent churches seek to focus on building for the future by making new places for new people.

Take a tour of your property, and ask yourself: *Is the signage, décor, and allocation of space primarily geared to the past or to the future? Is the sound equipment updated to assist the elderly hear better and equipped to allow newcomers to experience live-streaming video? Is the parking area geared to direct newcomers? Is your webpage non-churchgoer friendly? Is the language used in the worship service easily understandable for people who are seeking to become disciples of Christ?*

This approach is about more than just great customer service. Instead, it's mission-minded service that equips old-timers and newcomers with fresh expressions of faith that is needed. These fresh expressions can take many different forms; some traditional, some nontraditional, but both with a common purpose: to lead people into a meaningful relationship with Jesus Christ.

Resurgent churches do not throw out the baby with the bathwater, though. Rather, they expand the table of invitation for those who are already in membership and those who are seeking to become disciples of Christ.

Staffing to mature disciples. Staffing does not mean paid persons only. Volunteers—or as I prefer to call them, servant leaders—are essential to moving people through the stages of discipleship. The journey from being babes in Christ to exploring disciples of Christ to disciples of Christ to mature leaders in Christ requires a team of people who model, equip, teach, and transform people as they grow on their discipleship journey. Resurgent churches have an intentional plan of discipleship that navigates people through the process of spiritual maturity. This plan is developed in conjunction with the mission and vision of the leadership team.

A clear plan of developing worship attendees is essential to change the direction of a church. A discipleship plan works like a GPS, constantly assessing our position and directing us toward a preferred destination. Resurgence is a desired destination that has to be navigated with intentional strategies for developing people toward spiritual maturity.

Classes, small groups, online education, preaching, and stewardship all have to share a common message of maturing people for Kingdom service. Eugene Peterson, writing in *The Message* version of the Bible, makes this observation in Ephesians 4:11-14 (italics added):

He handed out gifts of apostle, prophet, evangelist, and pastor-teacher to train Christ's followers in *skilled servant work*, working within Christ's body, the church, until we're all moving rhythmically and easily with each other, efficient and graceful in response to God's Son, fully mature adults, fully developed within and without, fully alive like Christ. No prolonged fancies among us, please.

As we mature believers, resurgence will be the natural by-product of their maturity.

Systems to equip disciples. One of the hallmarks of vital ministry is a consistent process of on-boarding, training, mission alignment, accountability, leadership gifting, and discipleship benchmarking. The system or process that is created determines the ability of the ministry to grow to the next level.

Small-group training, coaching, teaching, and leadership development should be carefully aligned with the ministry vision and mission. But you don't have to start from scratch. There are numerous ministry conferences that take place annually where these strategies and proven best practices are taught. Networking with other ministries that are further along in the process than your ministry is another way to gain the needed expertise. But beware: Don't confuse good business models with good ministry models. A system that equips disciples must be first biblically based and spiritually driven because we are creating Christ followers.

Application

At the heart of making disciples is a commitment to lead people into a vibrant relationship with Jesus Christ. The tools and techniques of filling that task are varied and vast. From personal witnessing to systems that invite people into vital relationships, the primary objective of each is to remind people of the loving and saving grace of Jesus Christ.

This resource begins a conversation that moves ministries from accepting the status quo. People who love God and are willing to grow spiritually can create ministry environments that grow physically and spiritually. Resurgence begins as a mindset, an outlook, and an attitude toward God's preferred future and builds into creative, incremental improvements in ministry that brings people together and then sends them out to bring others.

Conclusion

We are ultimately in the business of making disciples of Jesus Christ for the transformation of the world. That happens with an invitation that inspires, informs, and equips disciples to serve Christ and the church. Resurgence is a process of retooling the church to engage the future with relevant strategies that connect people with God.

Action Item: We began this resource with seasons of change, and we will leave to the next season of resources not only bridges of hope but also drones of destiny. Our vantage point has evolved from an instant camera to a drone taking pictures from above. We are moving toward self-driven, automated systems of living. The church must be on the forefront of these innovations.

Man nor machine will phase out our ethnical input, moral balance, and spiritual disciplines. Resurgence invites incorporated proven strategies with emerging opportunities and still honors God in the process. Best practices and proven systems are good, but they will never replace the passion and purpose of a compelling God-given vision, one that transforms the hearts and minds of men and women who are willing to serve God by continuing to lead outposts of hope and transformation. Our preaching forms of delivery will change, but our core message must remain focused on inviting people to encounter Jesus Christ as their entryway into a relationship with God and His people.

Reflect and Respond

1. How do you evaluate the talent in your congregation?

2. Is your current disciple-making systems at your church relevant to the members you want to attract?

3. How often to you send your minsitry to developmental training?

4. Is your resurgence church currently teaching other churches on how God has continued to make your church relevant?

CHAPTER 9

Concluding Thoughts: Spiritual Leadership and Resurgence

"And I will give you shepherds according to my heart, who will feed you with knowledge and understanding."
— Jeremiah 3:15 (NIV)

Foundational for every Christian is to possess a heart toward God and leading and serving with a heart toward God's people.

Leadership Is Everything

The most important ingredient in congregational resurgence is leadership. There are thousands of resources that share programs and strategies for church leadership. Entire organizations have been created to craft and create leadership systems to be used in local church settings.

After 36 years of pastoral ministry, having served in new church starts, cross-cultural, suburban, and urban ministry settings, I (Rodney) know that there are universal principles and strategies that work in all leadership settings. Strategies and policies, while important, are only as effective as the skill of the leaders who implement them. Books, seminars, videos, podcasts, and leadership conferences are great at dispensing information; but transformation springs forth from learning, insight, experience, and implementation of effective tools administered by proven leaders.

Leadership is a gift, not just an office. Much of what we pass off as effective leadership is management. Leadership is a gifting that works because it is God-inspired, Holy Spirit-directed, and possesses an anointing that bears fruit. Gifted leaders thrive in most ministry settings. The core ingredients of effective pastoral leadership are listening, learning, loving, and lifting God's people to serve.

One of the cornerstones of effective leadership is equipping. Effective leaders must be learners, teachers, mentors, and coaches. Why? Because the primary tool for growing others is the ability to grow self. The evidence of self-growth is the fruit that is borne by the disciples and followers who then go on to equip others for service. In our modern setting, this level of leadership comes with mentoring, learning, and coaching.

Resurgence at every level of the church has a common thread running through it, and that thread is coaching. Coaching's main goal is to make persons self-aware. Coaching changes the narrative of leadership away from being "the expert" to lifting the skill set of all leaders and participants in ministry through self-awareness, cultural competency, and spiritual health for the local congregation.

The Book of Ephesians sets the tone for this when the apostle Paul set forth a growth environment that was defined with deeply embedded core values of education, maturation, and training. Resurgence has at its core a leadership culture that seeks to build on successful tradition and heritage but intentionally looks ahead toward innovation that addresses emerging needs of the church and the community.

"So Christ himself gave the apostles, the prophets, the evangelists, the pastors and teachers, to equip his people for works of service" Ephesians 4:11-16 (NIV).

Resurgence understands that the gifts of apostle, prophet, evangelist, pastor, and teacher are not only credentialed gifts but are also heart and head gifts. These gifts are given to men and women willing to be used by God to build unity and mature the saints for the work of ministry. Out of this awareness are birthed bold and courageous social movements that change homes and communities.

Resurgence in the black church begins and ends with understanding the "why." It is framed in the development of a leadership culture that has as its primary objective equipping others to serve God's kingdom. Throughout the ages, the church has thrived primarily because leaders have been clear about their "why." Our foreparents created faith communities to worship God, create disciplined followers of Christ, educate their children in faith, and to celebrate through vital worship a love of Christ and his church.

If we once again want to see the black church as an incubator of spiritual, cultural, economic, and social reform, we must heavily reinvest in leadership training for every aspect of society. Creating a culture of resurgence begins when we respond to the Scriptures' invitation to grow and mature spiritually. That involves leading people to reach unity in the faith and knowledge of the Son of God. Preaching and teaching must be anchored in these two life-giving objectives. We do this by reclaiming the importance of Christian education and spiritual formation.

To experience resurgence, churches must reprioritize the significance of spiritual formation for laity and clergy. Called and gifted teachers inspire greater worship attendance, increased commitment, generosity, and enthusiastic evangelistic outreach.

The second transformational element after knowledge is spiritual maturity. Maturity becomes evident in "measuring up to the full and complete standard of Christ" (Ephesians 4:13). In the black church, we value public worship as the primary indicator of a vital congregation. However, upon closer examination, vital, healthy, growing churches also possess a leadership culture that values spiritual formation and maturity as non-negotiable in the life of a congregation.

Resurgence is driven by a culture of maturing people for spiritual service. Creating discipleship systems that create and cultivate mature disciples is important to preparing mature leaders in the life of the church. This maturity is nurtured in the spiritual disciplines of prayer, study, worship, giving, and service. Maturing people for spiritual service will naturally and organically result in evangelistic outreach, increased financial generosity, expanded worship attendance, and greater involvement in ministry and missions.

The role of the church is changing to be more than just a preaching station. Growing and healthy congregations possess the tool to grow people into disciples of Jesus Christ for the transformation of the world. The tool is a well-crafted and implemented discipleship system.

What does this system look like? It begins with an assessment of the level of maturity of participants. That scale should progress from new believer to mature disciple of Christ. In addition to mission, vision, and core value statements, a discipleship system that moves people through the stages of being an inquirer, believer, new disciple, and mature disciple to becoming a multiplying leader must be present if resurgence is to occur.

Resurgence is more than just information. At its heart, it is transformation. Doing church differently at every level requires moving God's people to invest in a greater vision of holistic transformation. Just as technology has changed the way we communicate, resurgence provides a fresh perspective on how the church must reinvent itself to engage its community in new ways. At the heart of this movement is leadership that has as its primary objective innovative, transformative, and life-giving skills that equip and empower a new generation of leaders.

Leadership in today's church requires a culture of collaborative leading. Every growing leader needs to be connected with a network of resources that are constantly providing information, insight, inspiration, and innovative strategy to move ministry forward. These concepts then need to be incorporated into the emerging culture of local ministries. The church that only sees itself as a "once a week" worship center is obsolete. Resurgence demands that churches see themselves not solely as places of worship but also as disciple-makers focused on expanding their impact on the social, economic, educational, and political concerns of their respective communities.

Leadership invites us to reinvest in our own education and reeducation so that we are on the front lines of technology, finance, social trends, education, community empowerment, food and shelter opportunities, and affordable housing issues, just to name a few. Every church should be known by ministries that touch the community in positive ways. These opportunities are not without a biblical foundation that invites the church, while engaged in all of these activities, to make disciples of Jesus Christ.

Leadership mandates require that we not abandon the "why." Resurgence invites us to do all these things and more, ultimately so that God's kingdom on earth is honored and glorified by our witness.

Resurgence leadership is not just the top-down model of leadership. It is more about empowerment that includes two essential bookends: inspiring vision and effective communication. Resurgence places a high value on creating communities that are multidimensional and catalysts for diversity and engagement.

The church is uniquely able to live out this model because much of what we do is shaped out of transformation and the biblical story. And when woven together with God's story, this model motivates us to be the church, to be involved in mission, and to create community in response to who God calls us to be as redemptive community. Our mission therefore is not so much about ourselves as it is about the lives we impact for the cause of Christ.

The church becomes the sending point of resurgence, a place where fellow travelers gather to become equipped to go forth and make a difference in lives through service and witness. Leadership then becomes the underlying mission and purpose of ministry. We gather to learn, to lift, to lead, and to give life. Resurgence moves us from church meetings to ministry huddles. It moves us from "me and mine" to "us and theirs." Its leadership DNA is focused on relationship and ownership by all rather than by just a few.

Reflect and Respond

1. What does it take to create, spark, ignite, maintain, and sustain a resurgence in the church you attend, serve as a pastor, or serve as a lay leader?

2. As a church leader, do you fully understand whom and why you serve?

CONCLUSION

Resurgence is a life-long endeavor to improve the work of ministry. Vital ministries are driven by an ethic that seeks to keep the church moving forward in its nurture, outreach, evangelism, mission, education, and worship ministries.

In our conclusion, we realize that there are so many more stories to tell, strategies to suggest, and ideas to express. It is my (Rodney) hope that something that has been said within these pages invites you into "skilled servant work" in a way that honors God with your best and blesses the people you are called to serve.

I (Candace) am convinced of Jesus' words that "upon this rock I will build my church and the gates of hell won't prevail against it" (Matthew 16:18). Jesus is still calling and equipping the church to prevail! We must become the church we are called to be, not being content to be the church we have always been. Leaders and churches can retool for relevant, Spirit-led ministry that engages our communities. We can experience resurgence. I hope this resource helps you navigate your current ministry context well into the future.

CPSIA information can be obtained
at www.ICGtesting.com
Printed in the USA
FFHW021107250219
50650126-56066FF